Up & Running with Norton Utilities

Up & Running with Norton Utilities™

Rainer Bartel

SAN FRANCISCO • PARIS • DÜSSELDORF • LONDON

Acquisitions Editor: Dianne King
Translator: John Cantrell, Tristan Translations
Editor: Christian T.S. Crumlish
Technical Editor: Jon Forrest
Word Processor: Deborah Maizels
Book Designer: Elke Hermanowski
Screen Graphics Technician: Jeffrey James Giese
Typesetter: Deborah Maizels
Proofreader: Lisa Jaffe
Indexer: Ted Laux
Cover Designer: Kelly Archer
Screen reproductions produced by XenoFont

Library of Congress Card Number: 89-63174
ISBN: 0-89588-659-6

Manufactured in the United States of America
10 9 8 7 6 5 4 3 2 1

Up & Running

Let's say that you are comfortable with your PC. You know the basic functions of word processing, spreadsheets, and database management. In short, you are a committed and eager PC user who would like to gain familiarity with several popular programs as quickly as possible. The Up & Running series of books from SYBEX has been developed for you.

This clearly structured guide shows you in 20 steps what the product can do, how you make it work, and how soon you can achieve practical results.

Your Up & Running book thus satisfies two needs: It describes the program's capabilities, and it lets you quickly get acquainted with the program's operation. This provides valuable help for a purchase decision, along with a 20-step basic course that will give you a solid foundation in the program—even if you're a beginner with scant prior knowledge.

The benefits are plain to see. First, you'll invest in software that meets your needs because, thanks to the appropriate Up & Running book, you know the program's features and limitations. Second, once you purchase the product, you can skip the instruction manual and learn the basics of the program by following the 20 steps.

We have structured the Up & Running books so that the busy user spends little time studying documentation, and the beginner is not burdened with unnecessary text.

A clock shows your work time for each step. This indicates how much time you can expect to spend on each step with your computer.

Clock

Naturally, you'll need much less time if you only read through the steps rather than carrying them out at your computer. You can also save some time by scanning the short marginal notes to find the most important sections within a step.

Three symbols are used to highlight points of special note. These symbols and their meanings are shown below:

Symbols

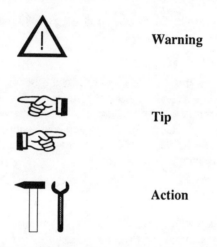

Warning

Tip

Action

An Up & Running book cannot, of course, replace a book or manual containing advanced applications. However, you will receive the information needed to put the program to practical use and to learn the basic functions.

Contents

The first step always covers software installation in relation to hardware requirements. You'll learn whether the program can operate with your available hardware. Various methods for starting the program are also explained.

The second step introduces the program's user interface.

The remaining 18 steps demonstrate basic functions, using examples or short descriptions. You'll also learn about various facilities for printing data, displaying it on the screen, and importing and exporting it. The last steps cover special program features such as a built-in macro language, additional editing facilities, or additional programs provided by third parties.The newest features of recently announced program versions are introduced to the extent possible.

An Up & Running book will save you time and money.

SYBEX is very interested in your reaction to the Up & Running series. Your opinions and suggestions will help all of our readers, including yourself.

Preface

Peter Norton became famous by taking advantage of the many shortcomings of the MS-DOS operating system. Norton's success as an author and as publisher of his famous Norton Utilities can be traced back to this simple fact. By 1982 he had made a name for himself as the author of a reference book that explained features of DOS that an average PC user would never learn from the manual.

He made an extensive study of floppy disks and hard disks and based the first Norton Utilities, which appeared at the end of 1982, on this study. These utilities were six independent programs, the most popular of which was called UE, or UnErase. With this program, you could restore unintentionally deleted files. The ability to unerase data follows directly from Norton's studies of PC disk management under MS-DOS.

Investigating disks

From the beginning, the Norton Utilities created great interest among PC enthusiasts. This very successful response turned a one-man operation into a company called Peter Norton Computing. In addition to several employees in sales and administration, the company included a new star programmer, John Socha. He enhanced Norton's first programs and created version 3.0. This version differed from its predecessor primarily in that it had a greatly improved user interface.

Norton Utilities 4.0 appeared on the market in 1986. The Advanced Edition followed in 1987. Versions 4.5 and 4.5 Advanced Edition have been available since the fall of 1988.

Current version 4.5

Up & Running with Norton Utilities covers versions 3.0, 4.0, 4.5 and the Advanced Editions of 4.0 and 4.5. The first step contains a table showing which programs each version contains and what the differences are. The introduction of each

Not all steps apply to every version

step specifies the versions covered in the step. You can skip any step that covers only versions you do not have.

If you do not yet own the Norton Utilities, you should study the first two steps in particular. These will help you decide whether you need the collection of programs. Otherwise, you should proceed through the steps in order.

After studying all 20 steps, you will be able to work with every program in the Norton Utilities without having to consult the original manual. You will be particularly well prepared to restore unintentionally erased data. I hope you enjoy Up & Running with Norton Utilities and I wish you lots of success at retrieving lost data!

Rainer Bartel, November 1989

Table of Contents

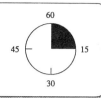
Since the Norton Utilities do not have to be specially custom-ized for the available hardware, they require no installation procedure in the usual sense. However, beginning with ver-sion 4.0, the Utilities have come with a program called INSTALL.EXE. This first step deals with that installation aid and specifies the hardware required to run the Norton Utili-ties. You will need 15 minutes for this step.

Preparations

Since working with original floppy disks always entails risk, it is important that you make backup copies before using the Norton Utilities.

Making Backup Copies

Each version comes with a different number of floppy disks. Version 4.5 is also available in 3-1/2-inch floppy disks.

Use the DOS command DISKCOPY to copy the original floppy disks. The command automatically formats each desti-nation floppy disk before copying. The 5-1/4-inch floppy disks in the Norton Utilities package are formatted for 360 K. If you have an AT with a 1.2 Mb drive, you should format the destination floppy disks using the following format command so that they will have the same format as the original disks:

```
FORMAT A:/4
```

Copy the label information from the original floppy disks to the labels of the destination disks. Store the original floppy disks in a safe place. For example, you can put them in

Preparing
labels

a separate disk box used exclusively to store original program floppy disks.

Installation on a Floppy Disk without INSTALL.EXE

If you have an older version, up to and including 3.1, you will not find any installation program on the program floppy disks. You will need to transfer the files manually.

If you have only one drive

The following procedure assumes that you have two floppy drives rather than a hard disk in your computer. If you only have one floppy drive (as in a Tandy 1000, for example), you will have to type A: in place of B:, and you will have to swap floppy disks more often.

1. Boot your computer with a system disk containing the DOS file FORMAT.EXE (or FORMAT.COM).
2. Insert a blank disk in drive B.
3. Format the new disk as a system disk with the command FORMAT B:/s.
4. Copy the AUTOEXEC.BAT and CONFIG.SYS files from the system disk to the formatted disk.
5. Insert the Norton Utilities program disk in drive A.
6. Copy all files from the program disk to the disk in drive B.

This will produce a Norton Utilities disk that you can use to boot the system. If you discover that you use this floppy disk often, you can enhance the AUTOEXEC.BAT file with a command that will call up the utilities directly.

You may follow a similar procedure to install versions 4.0 and 4.5 or their Advanced Editions on a PC without a hard disk. Unfortunately, not all the programs in these packages will fit on one 360 K floppy disk. The list below specifies the essential files for a floppy-drive based PC which also fit on a single 360 K floppy disk:

The most important programs

*   WIPEDISK.COM
*   WIPEFILE.COM
*   DI.EXE

- DS.EXE
- DT.EXE
- FA.EXE
- FI.EXE
- FS.EXE
- NU.EXE
- QU.EXE
- TM.EXE
- TS.EXE
- VL.EXE

Installation on a Hard Disk without INSTALL.EXE

The procedure for this installation is very simple. For this reason, the instructions are more terse:

1. Change to the root directory of the hard disk.
2. Create a directory for the Norton Utilities with the command MD NORTON.
3. Change to the new directory with the command CD NORTON.
4. Insert the Norton Utilities floppy disks into drive A, one after another, and copy the contents of each with the command COPY A:*.*.

Installation Using INSTALL.EXE

Version 4.5 contains an easy-to-use installation program that does not do much more than copy files. (It does include a few precautions and additional actions.) The program is interactive and does not need to be explained, but here are a few tips:

- Always specify a subdirectory of the root directory as the destination for the files you are copying. Incidentally, you may also enter the name of a new directory and the program will automatically create it.

- If you already have an older version of the Norton Utilities, you should choose the "Backup first" option. This option copies all old Norton Utilities files into a directory named NORTON.BAK.

- You should wait to modify the AUTOEXEC.BAT file directly until you are acquainted with the operation of the various programs. Select the "Skip to Next Step" option.

- Decline the offer to replace the original FORMAT.EXE program with the Norton Utilities program SF.EXE.

The Different Versions

Since this Up & Running book covers all versions starting with 3.0, you should look at Table 1.1 on the following page to determine which programs your version includes. The list also shows the steps that cover the various programs.

The Advanced Editions are identical to the corresponding standard versions, except that they contain additional programs. Since these additional programs are very useful, it is worth it to pay the higher price and buy the appropriate Advanced Edition.

Incidentally: As a registered owner of the Norton Utilities, you can upgrade to the current version for a modest charge.

Program	3.x	4.0 Adv.	4.0	4.5 Adv.	4.5	Step
BE				✓	✓	20
DI				✓	✓	3
DS	✓	✓	✓	✓	✓	10
DT	✓	✓	✓	✓	✓	5
FA	✓	✓	✓	✓	✓	14
FD				✓	✓	14
FF	✓	✓	✓	✓	✓	12
FI		✓	✓	✓	✓	14
FR			✓		✓	8
FS	✓	✓	✓	✓	✓	14
LD	✓	✓	✓	✓	✓	10
LP	✓	✓	✓	✓	✓	20
NCC				✓	✓	4
NCD		✓	✓	✓	✓	15
NDD				✓	✓	9
NI		✓	✓	✓	✓	2
NU	✓	✓	✓	✓	✓	17
QU		✓	✓	✓	✓	13
SA	✓	✓	✓			4
SD		✓			✓	9
SF				✓	✓	6
SI	✓	✓	✓	✓	✓	3
TM	✓	✓	✓	✓	✓	20
TS	✓	✓	✓	✓	✓	12
UD		✓	✓	✓	✓	11
VL	✓	✓	✓	✓	✓	7
WipeDisk	✓	✓	✓	✓	✓	7
WipeFile	✓	✓	✓	✓	✓	14

Table 1.1: Overview of the different versions

Step 2:
The User Interface

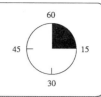

This second step is very short because it covers the user interface of the Norton Utilities, which has no real user interface. There is, instead, a consistent system of user guidance. This step will acquaint you with that system and also describe the Norton Integrator, which comes with versions 4.0 and 4.5.

Follow the examples to familiarize yourself with the system. This step only uses programs that cannot cause any damage. Allow 15 minutes.

The Screen Layout

One of the biggest differences between the 3.x generation and the 4.x generation of the Norton Utilities is in the screen layout. Whereas in older versions only the NU.COM program had its own screen template, in newer versions all of the interactive programs do. Compare Figures 2.1 and 2.2.

Step 17 covers the use of NU.COM in version 3.x in more detail.

The screens are of a rather plain design even in the more modern versions. Call up the Norton Utility program by entering the following:

Plain screens

        NU

As you can see, the program divides the screen into rectangular zones that each contain different information. The topmost lines display a copyright message, the date, and the time. Beneath this is a menu that you navigate using the cursor keys. That's all there is to the general screen layout of the Norton Utilities programs.

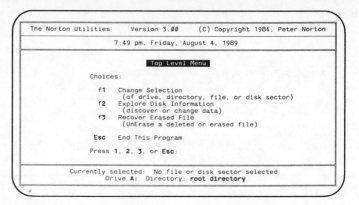

```
The Norton Utilities      Version 3.ØØ      (C) Copyright 1984, Peter Norton

                      7:49 pm, Friday, August 4, 1989

                              Top Level Menu
            Choices:

                f1   Change Selection
                      (of drive, directory, file, or disk sector)
                f2   Explore Disk Information
                      (discover or change data)
                f3   Recover Erased File
                      (UnErase a deleted or erased file)

                Esc  End This Program

                Press 1, 2, 3, or Esc:

            Currently selected:  No file or disk sector selected
                  Drive A:  Directory: root directory
```

Figure 2.1: The NU.COM version 3.0 opening screen

The Menus

For Norton Utilities 3.x, only the NU.COM program has a menu. Step 17 explains the operation of that program. Let's look at the NU.EXE program from version 4.0 or 4.5.

Example of menu operation

Let's use the main menu to try out some menu operation. It shows four items. A colored or bright bar highlights the first line. You can move this bar with the cursor keys to select any of the other three menu items. The following keys can be used to navigate the menu:

Key	Effect
↓	The bar moves to the next lower menu item.
↑	The bar moves to the next higher menu item.
→	The bar moves to the next lower menu item.
←	The bar moves to the next higher menu item.
PgDn	The bar moves to the bottom menu item.
PgUp	The bar moves to the top menu item.
End	The bar moves to the bottom menu item.
Home	The bar moves to the top menu item.

If you wish to execute a highlighted menu item, simply press the Return key.

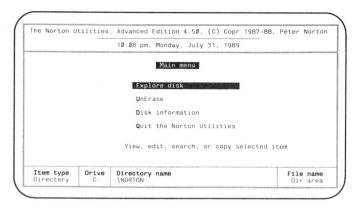

```
┌──────────────────────────────────────────────────────────────┐
│ The Norton Utilities, Advanced Edition 4.50, (C) Copr 1987-88, Peter Norton │
│                 10:08 pm, Monday, July 31, 1989                │
│  ┌────────────────────────────────────────────────────────┐   │
│  │                    ▓ Main menu ▓                        │   │
│  │                                                         │   │
│  │           ▓ Explore disk ▓▓▓▓▓▓▓▓▓▓▓▓▓▓▓▓▓             │   │
│  │                                                         │   │
│  │             UnErase                                     │   │
│  │                                                         │   │
│  │             Disk information                            │   │
│  │                                                         │   │
│  │             Quit the Norton Utilities                   │   │
│  │                                                         │   │
│  │          View, edit, search, or copy selected item      │   │
│  │                                                         │   │
│  ├────────┬───────┬──────────────────┬────────────────────┤   │
│  │Item type│ Drive │ Directory name   │       File name     │   │
│  │Directory│  C:   │ \NORTON          │       Dir area      │   │
│  └────────┴───────┴──────────────────┴────────────────────┘   │
└──────────────────────────────────────────────────────────────┘
```

Figure 2.2: The NU.EXE version 4.5 opening screen

Incidentally, the same key functions used in menus also apply to making selections in lists. You can test this immediately. Select *Explore disk* from the main menu and then select *Choose item* from the menu that follows. Selecting *File* from the next menu provides you with a list of the files in the current directory. You may now choose a file from this directory with the methods just described for selecting menu items.

Within the menu hierarchy, the Esc key moves you one level back. At this point, press the Esc key three times to return to the main menu.

The Esc key

There is an additional selection technique you should know. You have probably noticed that the initial letter of each menu line is either colored or brighter than the other letters in the line. If you type one of these letters, the program highlights the corresponding menu item and executes the appropriate function immediately. This shortcut works only for menus, and not for lists.

Key Functions

There are only a few fixed key functions that have the same effect for every program in the Norton Utilities. Among these are the key functions used in menu operations just mentioned. There are also two function keys that always work when a Norton Utilities program has its own screen.

You can call up a help message with F1. The help message will advise you about the program you are using. You can quit a program with F10. All other function key assignments differ from program to program.

The Norton Integrator

The Norton Integrator, a program that can be used to start all Norton Utilities programs, first appeared with version 4.0. The Integrator is helpful because it specifies all the necessary parameters for each program in an information window.

Run the Integrator from DOS with the following command:

```
NI
```

The Integrator divides the screen into three areas (see Figure 2.3). On the left is a rectangle containing an alphabetically sorted list of the Norton Utilities programs. Next to this on the right is an information window. The input line is across the bottom.

A colored or bright bar marks an entry in the program list. You already know how to move the bar, but the left arrow and right arrow cursor keys have no effect here.

As you page through the list, you will see that the information window displays explanations and that the highlighted program name also appears on the input line. You can execute the entry in the input line by pressing the Return key. If you wish to call a program without parameters, proceed as follows:

1. Highlight the desired program name.
2. Press the Return key.

If you call programs from the Integrator, you will automatically return to the Integrator after the program ends. For this reason, when working with this book, you should always use the Integrator (if you have it).

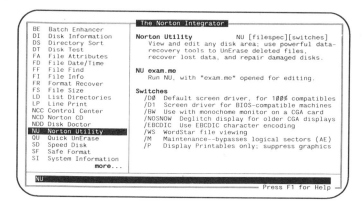

```
┌─────────────────────────────────────────────────────────────────┐
│                        ┤ The Norton Integrator ├                 │
│ BE  Batch Enhancer                                                │
│ DI  Disk Information    Norton Utility          NU [filespec][switches] │
│ DS  Directory Sort         View and edit any disk area; use powerful data- │
│ DT  Disk Test              recovery tools to UnErase deleted files, │
│ FA  File Attributes        recover lost data, and repair damaged disks. │
│ FD  File Date/Time                                                │
│ FF  File Find           NU exam.me                                │
│ FI  File Info              Run NU, with "exam.me" opened for editing. │
│ FR  Format Recover                                                │
│ FS  File Size           Switches                                  │
│ LD  List Directories    /D0   Default screen driver, for 100% compatibles │
│ LP  Line Print          /D1   Screen driver for BIOS-compatible machines │
│ NCC Control Center      /BW   Use with monochome monitor on a CGA card │
│ NCD Norton CD           /NOSNOW Deglitch display for older CGA displays │
│ NDD Disk Doctor         /EBCDIC Use EBCDIC character encoding     │
│ NU  Norton Utility      /WS   WordStar file viewing               │
│ QU  Quick UnErase       /M    Maintenance--bypasses logical sectors (AE) │
│ SD  Speed Disk          /P    Display Printables only; suppress graphics │
│ SF  Safe Format                                                   │
│ SI  System Information                                            │
│                more...                                            │
│ ┌──┐                                                              │
│ │NU│                                                              │
│ └──┘                                                              │
│                                            Press F1 for Help ══   │
└─────────────────────────────────────────────────────────────────┘
```

Figure 2.3: The Norton Integrator

Speed Search

Often, pressing cursor keys to page through a list can be a nuisance, particularly when the entry you are looking for is near the bottom. For this reason there is a technique called speed search for paging through long lists.

Press the Tab key once. The speed search message appears in the bottom right of the screen. Also, the entry disappears from the input line. You can begin to select a program by typing the first letter of its name, and the Integrator will automatically select the first entry in the list whose name begins with that letter. Try this now:

Start the speed search with Tab

1. Press Tab (if you have not already done so).
2. Type a **T**. The bar moves to the TM Time Mark entry.
3. Type an **S**. The bar moves to the TS Text Search entry.
4. Press the spacebar to end the speed search.

Think of the effort you have saved. To move from the topmost entry to the TS Text Search line, you must press the cursor key about twenty times. Using speed search, you only need to press four keys.

Parameters

This section explains how you tell the Integrator about parameters, but we will not yet discuss the parameters themselves.

The Integrator automatically appends a blank space to the program name displayed on the input line, and a cursor appears after the space. You start parameters with a slash (/) and then type specifications as explained in the information window.

Few
editing
capabilities

The input line can be edited, but only by erasing characters with the Backspace key. You delete one character to the left of the cursor each time you press the key, but you cannot delete the program name itself.

Step 3:

Testing Your System

When working on a PC, you often need to know the characteristics of the system. For this reason, among their many tools, the Norton Utilities contain two measuring instruments. The programs SI (System Information) and DI (Disk Information) measure the system performance.

You won't need either program for everyday PC use. But when a problem occurs, it can be very helpful to know, for example, just how much RAM your computer really has. You will need only about 15 minutes to try out both programs.

The SI Program

Almost every computer magazine uses the Norton measurement as an evaluation criterion. Those in the know might say, "The TAMPAQ 386x has a Norton SI of 23.4," to show that the computer in question is very fast.

The SI program measures the computer's operating speed. The core of the program is a number of small subprograms for the CPU to run. These subprograms contain mostly mathematical tasks of varying complexity. SI internally measures the time required for the CPU to execute these subprograms, but it does not gauge some features that are important for fast PCs, such as RAM access times.

SI measures the operating speed

The SI index compares the value determined to that of a reference PC, the original IBM XT. This machine was arbitrarily given an SI index of 1.0. If, for example, a fast 386 machine achieves a factor of 32.8, this means that it calculates 32.8 times faster than an IBM XT. Remember that this factor only reflects the CPU speed, and that SI does not always produce the same result in repeated tests.

Running SI

You run the program from the Integrator or by entering the following:

```
SI
```

Version 3.0 can only determine the pure computing index. Starting with version 4.0, you can also calculate the operating speed of a hard disk drive. To do this, you enter the code letter of the disk as a parameter, or switch, when starting the program, for example:

```
SI C
```

The program then also calculates the disk index (DI) and forms the average performance index (PI) from both values. You can use this number to compare the performances of different computers. In particular, SI displays the information shown in Table 3.1.

Category	Meaning
Computer name	Information about the manufacturer and computer type
Operating system	DOS version used
Built-in BIOS dated	Date the BIOS was finished
Main processor	CPU type
Co-processor	Coprocessor type—if present
Serial ports	Number of serial ports
Parallel ports	Number of parallel ports
Video Display Adapter	Type of video display adapter installed
Current Video Mode	Current video mode
Available Disk Drives	Number of drives available

Table 3.1: Information provided by the SI program

The numbers beneath the line "DOS reports 640 K-bytes of memory" show how much memory DOS and memory-resident programs occupy at present and how much RAM is still free. Under the heading "A search for active memory finds," you

will see information regarding video RAM and any available
extended memory.

Incidentally, do not be surprised if a different value appears
every time you run the SI program. Deviation of plus or minus 0.2 is normal and lies within the fault tolerance. Figure 3.1 shows a sample SI screen display.

```
      Operating System: DOS 3.30
    Built-in BIOS dated: Friday, March 3, 1989
         Main Processor: Intel 80386              Serial Ports: 1
           Co-Processor: None                   Parallel Ports: 2
  Video Display Adapter: Monochrome (MDA)
     Current Video Mode: Text, 25 x 80 Monochrome
  Available Disk Drives: 8, A: - H:

  DOS reports 704 K-bytes of memory:
       99 K-bytes used by DOS and resident programs
      605 K-bytes available for application programs
  A search for active memory finds:
      640 K-bytes main memory      (at hex 0000-A000)
      128 K-bytes display memory   (at hex A000-C000)
       32 K-bytes extra memory     (at hex C000-C800)
       80 K-bytes extra memory     (at hex CC00-E000)
    3,424 K-bytes expanded memory
  ROM-BIOS Extensions are found at hex paragraphs: C000 F000

    Computing Index (CI), relative to IBM/XT: 21.0
        Disk Index (DI), relative to IBM/XT: 7.0

  Performance Index (PI), relative to IBM/XT: 16.3

  C>
```

Figure 3.1: The result after running SI

The DI Program

You run the DI (Disk Information) program in the same way
as you do SI, optionally specifying the drive letter as a switch.
If you don't include a switch, the program investigates the
current drive. The information DI provides is mainly technical
in nature, but some of it can be of practical use.

DI compares the information provided by the operating system with what it determines from the boot sector. Taken together, these two sets of information supply a rather complete
picture of the floppy disk or hard disk being tested. Figure 3.2
shows the Disk Information screen.

The system ID indicates the DOS version used to format the
disk. This information will sometimes alert you to hard-disk
problems, such as would arise, for example, if someone formatted the hard disk with DOS 4.0 and you tried to operate

```
C>di
DI-Disk Information, Advanced Edition 4.50, (C) Copr 1987-88, Peter Norton

    Information from DOS          Drive C:          Information from the boot record
    ----------------------------------------------------------------------
                                     system id          'MSDOS3.3'
                                media descriptor (hex)        F8
                2               drive number
              512               bytes per sector             512
                4               sectors per cluster            4
                2               number of FATs                 2
              512               root directory entries       512
               64               sectors per FAT               64
           16,313              number of clusters
                                number of sectors         65,415
                1               offset to FAT                  1
              129               offset to directory
              161               offset to data
                                sectors per track             35
                                sides                         10
                                hidden sectors                35

C>
C>
```

Figure 3.2: DI provides this type of information

the disk with DOS 3.x. If a problem of this type occurs, you will have to reformat the disk using the DOS you have available, *after* you have made a backup copy.

Media descriptor

The media descriptor tells you the type of floppy disk or hard disk you have, using the codes explained in Table 3.2.

Code	Type
F0	1.4 Mb 3-1/2-inch floppy disk
F8	Hard disk
F9	1.2 Mb 5-1/4-inch floppy disk or 720 K 3-1/2-inch floppy disk
FD	360 K 5-1/4-inch floppy disk
FE	160 K 5-1/4-inch floppy disk
FF	320 K 5-1/4-inch floppy disk

Table 3.2: Media descriptor codes

Using DI, for example, you could identify a 1.2 Mb AT floppy disk that could no longer be formatted for 360 K.

The drive number is the sequential number specified by DOS. Drive A has the number 0, drive B the number 1, and so forth. The number of FATs can be interesting. (FAT stands for File Allocation Table.) Normally, DOS stores two copies on the disk. If DI shows only one FAT, there is something wrong with the disk, and you should reformat it (after backing up the data) to avoid any potential problems.

The remainder of the information is of little practical interest. Much of it is explained in the Norton Disk Companion, included with versions 4.0 and 4.5. This little 50-page book describes the technical basics of floppy disks and hard disks.

Step 4:

System Setup

This step covers the SA (Screen Attributes) program and the NCC (Norton Control Center) program. SA has been available since version 3.0. With version 4.5, NCC was added and SA was incorporated as a subcommand of the BE (Batch Enhancer) program. SA deals exclusively with screen presentation; NCC contains additional set-up facilities.

Changes you make to your screen will have no effect unless you add the ANSI driver into the CONFIG.SYS file. The ANSI driver makes it possible to drive the screen directly and is provided with DOS versions 2.x and later. Add the following line to the CONFIG.SYS file:

```
DEVICE=\DOS\ANSI.SYS
```

(In place of \DOS enter the name of the directory containing the ANSI.SYS file.)

The SA Program

You can change the representation of characters on the screen with SA, but only in text mode. You can run SA either from inside the Norton Integrator or directly from the DOS prompt. If you have version 4.5 you will have to use the command BE SA, instead of SA. When run from the DOS prompt, the program acts like a DOS command.

Always run SA with at least one switch. If you don't specify any, though, the program will list on the screen the switches it expects.

You can call SA with either one of three main commands or any number of a long list of switches. The main commands are

NORmal
REVerse
UNDerline

Abbreviating the switches for SA

You may abbreviate each switch using its first three letters. Say you enter the following:

    SA REV

(Remember, if you have version 4.5, you'll need to enter **BE SA REV.**) Following this, characters will be shown on the screen in reverse video (normally this means dark letters on a bright background, but for LCDs, it is usually the opposite of this). This command:

    SA NOR

will restore the customary display. If you use one of the main commands, you may not use any other switches. The following switches specify the intensity:

BRIght
BOLd
BLInking

Bright and *bold* are synonyms; bold is the more familiar term for owners of monochrome monitors. The following switches specify the foreground or background color:

WHIte
BLAck
RED
BLUe
GREen
CYAn
MAGenta
YELlow

You assign the foreground color by following the command directly with the appropriate switch; you assign the background color by typing *on* and then the switch. All of these switches are optional. If, for example, you do not wish to change the intensity, omit that switch. If you like the color of the background, only enter the foreground color. Incidentally, if you only specify one color, that color applies to the foreground unless you include *on*.

Here are a few examples and their effect:

SA BOLD YELLOW ON BLUE   Bright yellow letters on a blue background

SA BOLD   Bright letters—the foreground and background remain unchanged

SA ON WHI   White background—the foreground and intensity remain unchanged

SA BRI MAG ON BLA   Bright magenta letters on a black background

One last switch is important for owners of CGA and VGA adapters. You can prevent the color of the screen border from automatically taking on the color of the background with /N. EGA cards produce a picture without a border so for those cards the /N switch has no effect.

The NCC Program

Version 4.5 of the Norton Utilities includes the NCC program. With this program, you can change various system settings. The capabilities of the NCC can be divided into three groups covering these three areas:

- The display
- The keyboard and ports
- The date and time

You will see a list of capabilities on the left-hand side of the NCC window (Figure 4.1). You can highlight items from

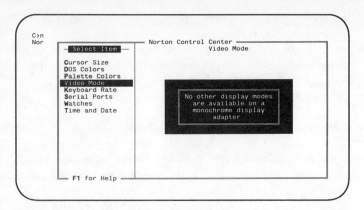

Figure 4.1: The Norton Control Center (NCC)

these choices in the usual manner. You select a program function with Return or the right arrow key, and then exit from the function with Return.

Key functions in the NCC

Exit the NCC with either the Esc key or F10. You can store the settings in a file by pressing the F2 key and then entering a name.

Let's say that you have stored your personal settings in a file called NCC.DAT. You can then recall the complete settings by entering the following:

```
NCC.DAT /SETALL
```

You can make individual settings separately by specifying other switches (e.g., /CURSOR).

The Display

Suppose you are unhappy with the shape of the cursor. This is a problem familiar to all laptop owners. Laptops usually show a small underline cursor that is very hard to see on the LCD screen. Let's say you want a large block cursor. You can make this change with the Cursor Size option.

Changing the cursor shape

A small box at the top right shows the existing cursor. The window for changing the shape is in the center. A pattern of bright or dark horizontal lines defines the cursor shape. You can now specify which of these lines you want turned on.

The topmost row, or line, bears the number 0, and the lowest row number depends on the graphics adapter you are using. It ranges from 7 (for CGA) to 15 (for VGA). On the left side of the center window is an arrow and a box containing the word Start (Figure 4.2). You can move this arrow with the up and down arrow keys. The arrow's position defines the first bright line of the cursor. The start box shows the number of that first line. The standard cursor starts in the second line from the bottom.To create a large block cursor, you can press the up arrow key until all the lines are lit.

The right arrow key moves you to the right side of the window. The arrow shown on this side specifies the bottom line of the cursor. You can move this arrow the same way. The box containing the word End will indicate the number of the last line. In order to achieve the described block cursor, you do not need to change the end line.

Play with this section of the program until you have found the cursor shape that you like. If you wish to revert to the default cursor, simply enter an asterisk (*).

If you choose the item *Video Mode*, the program will give you a selection of all the video modes permitted by your video

Setting the video mode

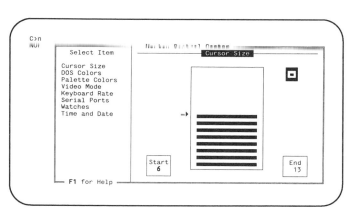

Figure 4.2: Specifying a cursor shape with the NCC

adapter. If, for example, you have a CGA card installed, you can choose between *25x80 black and white* and *25x80 color*. With a VGA card, you can also select more display lines.

The *DOS Colors* and *Palette Colors* items are available only with a color video adapter. If this adapter is set to black-and-white mode with the NCC, then you can only adjust the DOS colors.

DOS Colors specifies the colors for the foreground, background, and border. This feature is left over from earlier SA program versions. However, you can make the changes in the NCC in a very intuitive fashion because you'll immediately see the effects on a small display.

Palette Colors is somewhat more difficult to understand and is only of interest for owners of EGA and VGA cards. These two adapters are able to display 16 colors at once, numbered consecutively from 0 to 15. (Some VGA adapters can display even more colors but the NCC can only edit 16.) Each color has a palette of 64 available hues. From these hues, you can select the one that will be displayed under the number and name of the appropriate DOS color.

Experimenting with the controls will make these options more clear. This time, you can even see the effect on the entire screen. The NCC covers only a portion of the screen and the background immediately displays your color settings.

Keyboard and Ports

You can set the keyboard repetition rate with the *Keyboard Rate* item. In the top section, move the marking on the scale between Slow and Fast using the right and left arrow keys. The program displays the speed in characters/second and the standard is 10.0 characters per second.

Press the down arrow cursor key to move to the area for setting the Delay Before Auto Repeat. Here you set the delay time before a key being held down starts to repeat. The scale extends from Short to Long and displays the time delay in tenths of a second. The normal value is 0.5 second.

The input line bearing the name Keyboard Test Pad can be used for trying out your settings.

Incidentally, you can return to the initial settings here, too, by typing an asterisk (*). Exit this section of the program with the Return key.

You can set the switches for your serial port(s) under the item *Serial Ports*. This item corresponds to the DOS command MODE COM1....

Date and Time

The last two menu items concern date and time. *Time and Date* is used to set the system time and date. Move within a setting line with the left arrow and right arrow keys. Switch between date and time with the up and down arrows.

You can change each highlighted field with the + and – keys. Increase a value by pressing + and decrease it with –. You may also enter values manually. The program does not accept invalid input. If you enter something invalid and try to exit this section, the initial values will reappear.

Figure 4.3 shows the four stopwatches available under the item *Watches*. They can be used with the TM (Time Mark) program (see Step 20); however, you may also use them

Setting the stop-watches

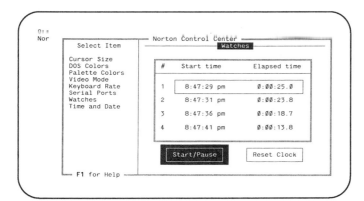

Figure 4.3: The four stopwatches in the NCC

simply as timers. Switch between *Start/Pause* and *Reset Clock* with the left arrow and right arrow keys. Select one of the four watches with the up and down arrows.

Step 5:

Testing Your Disks

Physical defects cause many of the problems that can plague a floppy disk or hard disk. Such physical defects are usually mechanical damage to the medium, sometimes even magnetic disturbances, and, in rare cases, genuine product defects.

With the DT (Disk Test) program introduced in this step, you will be able to find physical defects, possibly repair them, and block areas recognized as damaged. Whenever problems occur with the data medium, you should always first analyze the medium with DT. You cannot put the repair programs to good use until you have done so.

Step 5 requires about 15 minutes. If you follow the example using a damaged floppy disk, you may need somewhat longer.

The DT Program

The Norton Utilities have included DT since version 3.0, and it has retained its original user interface. This means that it does not have its own screen, but rather runs directly from DOS. You can specify additional switches to investigate particular directories and files. The ability to repair defective areas or render these areas unusable has only been available since version 4.0.

Defective Floppy Disks

If you in fact want to try DT out in a serious way, you should intentionally damage a floppy disk. Then you can learn how a serious physical defect is spotted by analyzing the defective disk.

Take a floppy disk that you will no longer need. Format the floppy disk and copy a few files to it. Check whether the floppy disk can be read by calling up the directory. How you damage the floppy disk is best left up to your imagination. You could put a staple through the disk (and then remove it, so as not to damage the drive). You could also use a hole punch or a thumbtack to make a hole in the disk.

Note! Make sure there is no foreign matter attached to the floppy disk when you insert it into the drive! Also, smooth out any unevenness in the disk's surface before you test the disk.

Starting DT

You start the program either from the Integrator or directly from the DOS command level (Figure 5.1). You must specify the drive and at least one of the following switches: /D, /F, or /B. /D stands for "disks," /F means "file" and the /B indicates "both." If you specify /D, the program analyzes the entire disk by cluster, regardless of whether files occupy these clusters or not. Specifying /F causes the program to test files and directories. You may combine the analyses by using the /B switch.

Starting with version 4.0, you can specify a directory or file name instead of the drive name, and thereby restrict the analysis to smaller units.

Insert the damaged floppy disk in the drive and run DT as follows:

```
DT A:/B
```

You may use a variation like the one below if you have version 4.0 (or later):

```
DT A:\DOS\FORMAT.EXE /F
```

In version 3.0, you receive a report on the condition of the floppy disk following the command. You may print out this report or store it in a file. To do either, you must enter additional switches, for example,

```
DT A:/B/LOG > PRN
```

```
C>dt a: /b
DT-Disk Test, Advanced Edition 4.50, (C) Copr 1987-88, Peter Norton

During the scan of the disk, you may press
BREAK (Control-C) to interrupt Disk Test

Test reading the entire disk A:, system area and data area
  The system area consists of boot, FAT, and directory
    No errors reading system area

  The data area consists of clusters numbered 2 - 355
    No errors reading data area

Test reading files
  Directory A:\
    No errors reading files
C>
C>
C>
C>
C>
C>
C>
```

Figure 5.1: How DT reports on intact floppy disks

for sending the output to the printer, or

```
DT A:/B/LOG DTEST.DAT
```

to store the result in the file DTEST.DAT.

Messages

During the test run, DT may output various error messages. From these messages, you can determine whether the problem can be solved. Each message first reports the number of the "bad cluster" it has found. Figure 5.2 shows some error messages generated by a defective disk. Below are the possible messages and their meanings.

Defective clusters

NO DANGER	The cluster has already been marked as defective and is no longer used for storage.
DANGER TO COME	The cluster is damaged but not yet occupied by a file. It should be marked as damaged.
DANGER NOW	The cluster is defective and is being used by a file. The file in jeopardy can be copied to an intact area.

```
During the scan of the disk, you may press
BREAK (Control-C) to interrupt Disk Test

Test reading the entire disk A:, system area and data area
  The system area consists of boot, FAT, and directory
    No errors reading system area

  The data area consists of clusters numbered 2 - 355
    338th cluster read error: already marked as bad; no danger
    339th cluster read error: already marked as bad; no danger
    340th cluster read error: already marked as bad; no danger
    341st cluster read error: already marked as bad; no danger
    342nd cluster read error: already marked as bad; no danger
    347th cluster read error: already marked as bad; no danger
    348th cluster read error: already marked as bad; no danger
    349th cluster read error: already marked as bad; no danger
    350th cluster read error: already marked as bad; no danger
    351st cluster read error: already marked as bad; no danger

Test reading files
  Directory A:\
    No errors reading files

C>
```

Figure 5.2: How DT reports on defective floppy disks

In versions 4.0 and 4.5, if the program finds bad clusters, you can have it automatically mark them after the test. To do so, start DT with the /M switch. Then answer the question "Errors found in disk areas not currently in use - Mark them as bad sectors, to prevent use (Y/N)?" with **Y**.

Application

What can you do when you know that your data medium is physically damaged? Follow the instructions below for a floppy disk in drive A (only for versions 4.0 and 4.5):

1. Start DT by entering **DT A:/B/M**.
2. After the first pass, when DT offers to mark the damaged clusters, answer **Y**.
3. In the second pass, DT will copy the jeopardized files onto undamaged areas if this is possible. If the disk does not have the capacity, the program will report this.
4. Copy the contents of the damaged disk to an intact data medium.
5. Throw the defective floppy disk away!

If all the files can not be copied onto intact areas because of a lack of space, you may lose some data. However, files that use bad clusters can often be copied correctly in spite of this. If you test a hard disk using the /M switch, and DT reports bad clusters and marks them, you need not worry. To be extremely safe you could make a backup of the hard disk and then reformat it, but this is hardly necessary.

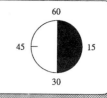
This step covers SF (Safe Format), a program first provided with version 4.5 of the Norton Utilities. It is intended to replace the MS-DOS format program. The Norton Utilities version 4.5 installation program goes so far as to offer to replace FORMAT.EXE with SF.

Allow at least 30 minutes to work with SF.

The SF Program

The idea for this program came from Norton employees who heard from customers about failed attempts at data recovery. The cause of the data loss was usually an unintentional format of the data disk.

When formatting, MS-DOS destroys important traces of old files. The SF program—as implied by the name Safe Format—takes another tack, keeping a copy of the old FAT (File Allocation Table) during formatting. Both QU (Quick UnErase) and NU (Norton Utilities) can recover data stored on the disk before the last format using this FAT.

*Safe
formatting*

SF also provides a lot of other convenient features not offered by its MS-DOS counterpart, FORMAT.EXE.

You can start the program from the Integrator or directly from the MS-DOS prompt. You may specify various switches that require special settings at the start. This is not necessary as a rule, however, because SF runs in its own window and you have access to all the options through menus.

The capacity switches correspond to those used by MS-DOS. Of these, the most important capacity switch is /4. With it, you can format a 5-1/4-inch floppy disk for 360 K in an AT drive.

Starting SF

You must, of course, first specify the drive containing the disk to be formatted. Insert a new floppy disk (or one containing files you no longer need) in drive A and start the Norton Integrator. Then, select the SF program and enter **A:** as the input-line parameter. Start the program by pressing Return.

The left half of the SF window contains current information regarding the program and the control menu (Figure 6.1). Beneath the Configuration Options heading appear the switch settings that you may have made.

If you start SF only specifying a drive, this screen displays several items. It shows the drive letter and, if relevant, floppy disk capacity (e.g., 1.2M for an AT drive). It also indicates whether this is a bootable system disk (for possible future use), displays a label that may be given to the disk, and shows the format mode.

You can change the specifications using the menu. Let's assume you want to make the floppy disk a 360 K system disk

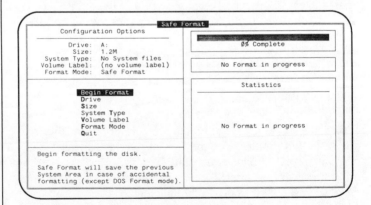

Figure 6.1: The SF (Safe Format) program

capable of booting the computer. Proceed as follows to accomplish this:

1. Select the *Size* menu item.
2. In the following window, select the *360K* menu item.
3. Select the *System Type* item.
4. In the following window, select the *System Files* item.
5. Select the *Begin Format* menu item.

Once you have done this, the program will format the floppy disk and copy the system files. During this procedure, some actions depend on the format mode selected.

Format Modes

Select the *Format mode* option. You'll see the following four choices:

- Safe Format
- Quick Format
- DOS Format
- Complete Format

The simplest mode is DOS Format. It is no different from formatting with the corresponding MS-DOS command. The progress display during the format is interesting.

In the top area, a bar displays the percentage of formatting accomplished. Below this, SF specifies which read/write head and which track is now being formatted. Under Statistics, you will find a time estimate and the actual elapsed time. In addition, the program displays the total number of sectors, the formatted number of sectors, and a cumulative display of defective sectors. The bottom four lines correspond to the message that FORMAT.EXE produces at the end of formatting. (See Figure 6.2).

Statistics displayed

Safe Format mode only takes slightly longer than using FORMAT.EXE. In this mode, the program first analyzes the floppy disk and issues a warning if data is already present on the disk. You then have the opportunity to abort the format.

```
┌──────────────────────────── Safe Format ─────────────────────────┐
│   Configuration Options           ┌──────────────────────────────┐ │
│                                   │        0% Complete           │ │
│      Drive:  A:                   └──────────────────────────────┘ │
│       Size:  1.2M                  ┌──────────────────────────────┐ │
│ System Type: No System files      │    No Format in progress     │ │
│ Volume Label: (no volume label)   └──────────────────────────────┘ │
│ Format Mode: Safe Format                                           cs │
│        Beg ┌──────────────────────────────────────┐               │ │
│        Dri │ This diskette may contain data        │   00:14:19   │ │
│        Siz │ Are you sure you want to format it?    │   00:00:05   │ │
│        Sys │                                        │              │ │
│        Vol │          ┌─────┐                       │      2,400   │ │
│        For │          │ Yes │  No                    │         30   │ │
│        Qui │          └─────┘                       │          1   │ │
│            └──────────────────────────────────────┘               │ │
│                                    Total Disk Space:  1,213,952   │ │
│                                        System Space:         0    │ │
│                                    Bad Sector Space:         0    │ │
│     Press ESC to cancel formatting   Available Space:  1,213,952  │ │
│                                                                    │ │
└────────────────────────────────────────────────────────────────────┘
```

Figure 6.2: SF shows the work in progress

If you continue formatting, the program first saves the data found (in particular, a copy of the old FAT). Only then does the program format the disk. The actual formatting operation runs at roughly twice the speed of the MS-DOS operation. It is even quicker with Quick Format—particularly with disks that have already been formatted. For such disks, SF formats (i.e., releases for data storage purposes) only those areas previously occupied by data. For a 1.2 Mb floppy disk that is, for example, three-quarters empty, the formatting process will take only about 2 seconds.

Time advantage of Quick Format

Quick Format saves you time, except with brand new floppy disks. The Complete Format option takes longer because this option not only executes the standard Safe Format process but also completely erases all areas occupied by data. In a sense, the Complete Format option is a combination of Safe Format, FORMAT.EXE, and WipeDisk.

Other Settings

You can specify the drive containing the disk you wish to format with the *Drive* option. Use caution! The hard disk can also be formatted unintentionally this way. While, as a rule, all data can be restored—the recovery operation takes time and a toll on your nerves. Therefore, only format the hard disk in an extreme emergency, and back up your hard disk regularly.

You can set floppy disk capacity with *Size*. If you do so, you will see the data capacity choices that your drive and controller can format. You cannot unintentionally format a 3-1/2-inch disk for 360 K. The *System Type* option makes it possible for you to copy system files to a floppy disk. You can also leave space for these files (with the *Leave space* option) and copy the system files later with the DOS SYS command or make the entire disk capacity available for data.

Under *Volume Label*, you can specify a name for the floppy disk. When you analyze the floppy disk with NU, it displays this name. As you have seen, you start formatting with *Begin Format*. You can interrupt this operation at any time with the Esc key. Exit the SF program with *Quit*.

Floppy disk capacity

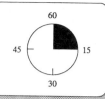

Hard Disk Editing

This step covers two programs used to edit the hard disk. You use VL (Volume Label) to change the disk name and Wipe-Disk to erase the entire disk. Both programs come with all versions and differ only slightly from version to version.

Since you are unlikely to use either program very often, you only need 15 minutes to quickly work through this step.

The VL Program

Under MS-DOS, you can specify a name comprising up to 11 characters for every hard disk, floppy disk, and partition. This name only plays a role during formatting. Under MS-DOS (from 3.3 on) every attempt to format a hard disk or a hard disk partition results in a question such as "Enter volume label for drive C:". You can only start formatting if you know the disk name.

Note: Do not try to format the hard disk! Not all DOS versions ask that question!

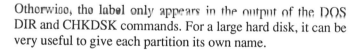
Otherwise, the label only appears in the output of the DOS DIR and CHKDSK commands. For a large hard disk, it can be very useful to give each partition its own name.

The DOS LABEL command also allows you to assign a name to a disk or partition. The difference between LABEL and the VL program is that with LABEL you may use only upper-case letters and no special characters at all. VL allows you to use all characters that can be entered from the keyboard, even blanks. It is always best to start VL with the required switches directly from the Integrator. The first switch should be the drive letter, of course. The second is the name that you wish to assign.

If you want to use blanks in the name you assign, you must enclose the name in quotation marks. Otherwise, quotation marks are unnecessary. In order to assign the name "* TEST *" to the hard disk in drive C, you must enter the following:

```
VL C: "* TEST *"
```

If you do not specify a name when running the program, the program shows the old name and allows you to abort the process if you wish.

The WipeDisk Program

You use WipeDisk for data security. There is a story about a well-known lawyer whose office recently sold two used PCs, each equipped with a hard disk. Before the sale all data was removed from the disks with the DOS DEL command. A technically sophisticated PC user got hold of one of the units and resurrected all the data previously stored on the hard disk, using the Norton Utilities. By doing this, he obtained highly confidential information about the lawyer's clients.

The WipeDisk program would have prevented that security breach. This program not only erases all data but also writes over all sectors of the disk with an arbitrary value you can select. This process is so secure that the Department of Defense (DoD) has expressly approved it. (After all, it's based on DoD data security guidelines.)

You should use this program with extreme caution. Data eliminated by a WipeDisk pass cannot be restored. For this reason, be very careful!

You can specify five switches:

/E   The program overwrites only unused areas of the disk.

/G3   The program overwrites the disk three times in accordance with DoD regulations. In place of 3, you may insert any value between 1 and 99.

/LOG>PRN	The program redirects all messages occurring during a pass to the printer.
/LOG>LOG.DAT	The program redirects all messages occurring during the pass into the file LOG.DAT.
/R1	The program overwrites the disk once. You may use any value between 1 and 99.
/V0	The program overwrites the sectors with the ASCII character having the code 0. Instead of this, you may specify any value between 1 and 255.

Following a WipeDisk pass, the disk will no longer be capable of storing files. You must first reformat it.

Step 8:

Disk Maintenance

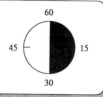

This step introduces the NDD (Norton Disk Doctor) and SD (Speed Disk) programs. NDD is a combination of Disk Test (DT) and the Norton Utility (NU) that comes only with version 4.5. SD comes with the Advanced Editions of versions 4.0 and 4.5.

With the Disk Doctor, you can perform preventive maintenance on floppy disks and hard disks. In an emergency, you can sometimes even fix them. The results can be astonishing. When a floppy disk is so severely damaged that DOS displays a "General failure..." type of message, it means that, according to DOS standards, attempts at recovery are futile. NDD often proves the opposite.

For testing the program in this step, you should use the floppy disk you intentionally damaged for the fifth step, if you did not discard it. Then, you can learn how to speed up your hard disk with Speed Disk. Budget about 30 minutes for this step.

The NDD Program

As usual, you can run the NDD program from the Integrator or from DOS. You must specify the drive of the disk to examine. If you do not specify a drive letter, the program automatically selects the current drive.

Additional switches specify the scope of work and the output of a log. With the /QUICK switch, the Disk Doctor restricts its attention to the system area of the data medium. You should use this method whenever a system disk does not work. The /COMPLETE switch has the program automatically diagnose and fix both the system area and the data area.

Two operating modes

With the /R:NDD.LOG switch (for which you can specify any file name in place of NDD.LOG), the program stores a log of the NDD run in the specified file. /RA:NDD.LOG appends the current log to an already existing file named NDD.LOG. You can use these switches to make a continuing status report of your data medium.

Running NDD Automatically

Insert the damaged floppy disk in drive A again, and start the program with the following:

```
NDD A:/COMPLETE
```

Figure 8.1 shows NDD running. The program first checks all available drives. Now and then, NDD reports during this process that the type of hard disk is not correct. It determines this by checking the disk ID. The NDD internal list can not possibly include all conventional disk types, so you can usually ignore messages of this type. You should only check the setting if real problems occur with the hard disk—for example, if DOS no longer recognizes it. In AT compatibles, the hard-disk type is usually stored in battery-backed CMOS RAM. The contents of this RAM can be changed with a special setup program.

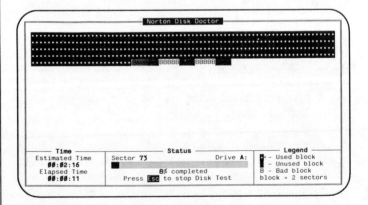

Figure 8.1: The Norton Disk Doctor (NDD)

If you confirm the message displayed by pressing the Return key, nothing seems to happen for a while. During this time, NDD studies the controller of the designated drive and selects one of the analysis methods based on the information found. Normally, the following three phases occur one after another:

- The program analyzes the DOS boot sector.
- The program analyzes the FAT (File Allocation Table).
- The program analyzes, and handles if necessary, each individual sector or cluster.

Sequence of operations

The treatment corresponds to the method you already know from DT (Disk Test). The program marks bad clusters and copies any data affected by such damage to intact areas.

As already mentioned, this process runs fully automatically with the /COMPLETE switch. For this reason, you should have NDD produce a report of the results. To do this, when starting NDD in automatic mode, you should always use the /R:NDD.LOG switch. The program then stores the results in a text file. You can print out the text file by typing the following:

```
PRINT NDD.LOG
```

Or you can view it on the screen (Figure 8.2) by typing this:

```
TYPE NDD.LOG
```

If you specify the report switch in the form /RA:NDD.LOG, the program appends each new report to the last stored report.

This report contains two types of information with which you are already familiar—Logical Disk Information and Physical Disk Information. Both of these are identical to the corresponding information produced by DT. Even the status information is similar to that of the DT program.

Two types of information

If you work with NDD, you will probably stop using DT because the Disk Doctor is much easier to use.

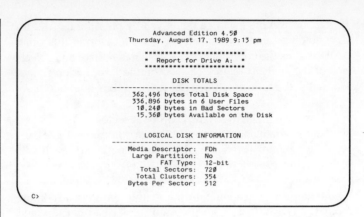

```
              Advanced Edition 4.50
        Thursday, August 17, 1989 9:13 pm

        *************************
        *  Report for Drive A:  *
        *************************

                  DISK TOTALS
        ---------------------------------------
          362,496 bytes Total Disk Space
          336,896 bytes in 6 User Files
           10,240 bytes in Bad Sectors
           15,360 bytes Available on the Disk


             LOGICAL DISK INFORMATION
        ---------------------------------------
          Media Descriptor:  FDh
          Large Partition:   No
                 FAT Type:   12-bit
             Total Sectors:  720
            Total Clusters:  354
           Bytes Per Sector: 512

  C>
```

Figure 8.2: An NDD report

Running NDD Interactively

Start NDD again without any switches. Just include the disk drive designation A: when running the program. This time, the process does not start automatically. Instead, the program presents you with its main menu. This menu allows you to choose among three options.

At this point, select *Diagnose Disk*. In the following window, you can select the desired drive. On the screen, you will see that the program has highlighted the drive you specified when starting it (Figure 8.3). You can confirm this selection with the Return key.

If you want to analyze several drives one after another, you can mark several lines with the spacebar. The program indicates each selection with a check mark at the beginning of the line.

You can also erase these markings with the spacebar. In this sample run, you should restrict your attention to the A: drive. When you have selected a floppy disk drive, the program requests that you insert the disk to be analyzed.

The program then analyzes the floppy disk according to the procedure outlined above. You can read the logical and physical information about the disk in two windows. You can then confirm that the entire floppy disk is to be analyzed.

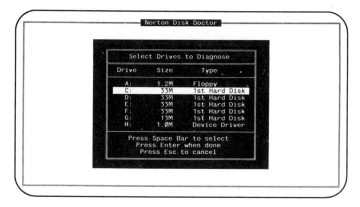

```
┌─────────────────── Norton Disk Doctor ───────────────────┐
│                                                           │
│   ┌─────────────────────────────────────────┐            │
│   │       Select Drives to Diagnose          │            │
│   │  Drive    Size      Type                 │            │
│   │   A:      1.2M     Floppy                │            │
│   │   C:       33M     1st Hard Disk         │            │
│   │   D:       33M     1st Hard Disk         │            │
│   │   E:       33M     1st Hard Disk         │            │
│   │   F:       33M     1st Hard Disk         │            │
│   │   G:       13M     1st Hard Disk         │            │
│   │   H:      1.0M     Device Driver         │            │
│   │                                          │            │
│   │      Press Space Bar to select           │            │
│   │      Press Enter when done               │            │
│   │      Press Esc to cancel                 │            │
│   └─────────────────────────────────────────┘            │
│                                                           │
└───────────────────────────────────────────────────────────┘
```

Figure 8.3: The drive selection window in NDD

Next you are asked to choose whether bad clusters are to be marked automatically or only after your confirmation. You should use the automatic mode, so select the No answer. During the run, the program will mark bad clusters and copy affected data to intact areas. The program displays, at the bottom left, an estimate of how long the run will last and how much time has elapsed. When the program finishes, it displays a status report on the screen. You can have this report written to a file.

Marking bad clusters

After returning to the main menu, you can either exit NDD (by selecting the *Exit Disk Doctor* option) or select *Common Solutions*. Under this item, you'll find a choice of three methods that can be used to solve frequently occurring floppy-disk and hard-disk problems.

These are the three options available if you choose the *Common Solutions* menu item:

- Make a Disk Bootable
- Recover from DOS's RECOVER
- Revive a Defective Diskette

Making a Disk Bootable

You already know that you can make a disk bootable during formatting by specifying the /S switch. Only a disk formatted in this manner can accommodate DOS system files. It often occurs, however, that you later want to convert a disk into a system disk. You can do this with the DOS SYS command only if the disk in question was once formatted with the /S switch. If this is not the case, DOS issues an error message when attempting to copy system files with the SYS command.

Space for
the system
files

You can prepare a bootable system disk with the *Make a Disk Bootable* option. This assumes that there is enough space available for the three system files. (For MS-DOS 3.3, there must be about 80 K free, for example.) DOS stores data in the boot sector of a floppy disk that has not been formatted as a bootable disk. NDD copies that data from the boot sector to another area of the floppy disk and then copies the necessary information to the boot sector.

You won't need to do anything during this process unless there is not enough space for the system files. If this is the case, you'll have to exit from the process and the NDD program, and then delete a few files from the floppy disk to make the necessary space available.

Recovering from RECOVER

If, as every sensible PC owner does, you occasionally make a backup of your hard disk, you are prepared for the worst case—a head crash with a total loss of data. If this happens, you can use the DOS RECOVER command, which copies the files created with the DOS BACKUP command from the backup medium onto the hard disk.

DOS
RECOVER
command

During this recovery process, however, the directory structure is usually reproduced incorrectly and your disk is left a tangled mess. You can avoid such a mess from the outset if you reconstruct the disk with this NDD option instead of with the DOS RECOVER command. But even if you have run RECOVER, you can still straighten out the chaos with this option.

When RECOVER runs, it renames all files and puts them in the root directory. You must then manually rename these files and directories later with the correct names.

Reviving a Defective Diskette

If DOS issues its infamous "General failure..." error message, recovery is not possible at all without NDD. Several problems can cause this message. Unless the boot and FAT sectors are physically damaged, these problems can usually be fixed.

The *Revive a Defective Diskette* option attempts to make all undamaged sectors usable again and often fixes the boot sector during the process. Unfortunately, this revival usually results in an irreversible loss of data, even with the help of other Norton Utilities. Therefore, you should really only use this option in an extreme emergency.

The SD Program

For some time now, optimization programs for hard disks have been in vogue. They owe their existence to the clever storage method DOS uses. DOS does not store files in consecutive sectors, but rather in sectors that are free at that moment. Storage begins with a free sector and continues in the next free one. The information about which sectors are being used to store which files is contained, among other places, in the FAT.

Optimizing a hard disk

How does DOS know which sectors are free? The FAT contains this information also. Deleted files are not actually erased; their entries in the FAT are changed. (Incidentally, this principle is the basis for data recovery programs.)

Because the free and occupied sectors occur haphazardly, the sectors of a single file are often distributed over the entire hard disk. When reading such files, the read/write head must therefore move back and forth regularly. This takes time. For this reason, the hard disk becomes slower the more it fills up and the more often reading, writing, and deletion operations are executed.

The Speed Disk program automatically copies the data of each file into consecutive sectors. In addition, it arranges the files on the disk in size order.

This program can be started from the Integrator or from DOS.

You need not specify any switches. If you do not specify a drive, SD works on the current drive. There are various switches available, but these will be described later because SD can operate interactively.

SD's working screen contains four areas. At the bottom right, you'll find an explanation of the symbols used in the graphic representation of the disk in the main area. The status field shows how far the optimization process has progressed. There is a menu at the bottom left. Start the process with the *Optimize Disk* option. *Exit Speed Disk* ends the program. You can select a different disk (or an additional partition of a subdivided hard disk) with *Change Drive*.

Before starting the optimization process, you can see whether optimization is necessary at all. To do so, select the *Disk Statistics* option. The customary basic information is output in a window. The most important line is the one specifying "Percent of unfragmented files." This value will help you decide whether optimization makes sense. If the percentage is greater than 95%, running SD is a waste of time.

The specifications regarding cluster status can also be interesting. If you see here that the number of "clusters allocated to movable files" considerably exceeds the number of "unused (free) clusters," you can prepare yourself for the optimization process taking a long time. If the number of free clusters is very low (less than 500), it may be that optimization will not help at all.

Setting the Options

Return to the main menu. Now select *Set Options*. Here you find the tools for fine tuning the program. First select *Optimization Method*. The options have the following meanings:

Complete Optimization	The program uses all applicable methods.
File Unfragment	The program uses only the described method of producing contiguous files.

Quick Compression	The program fills empty clusters so that all empty clusters are located on the end of the disk (where the highest cluster numbers are). This also provides a certain increase in speed.
Only Optimize Directories	The program only optimizes directory entries. The information regarding the available directories is where it is easy to access.

You will rarely want to choose an option other than *Complete Optimization.*

Return to the Set Options menu. You can specify a sequence for the directories with *Directory Order.* During optimization, the program sorts most of the directories alphabetically. But it places the directories containing the Norton Utilities and the DOS commands first. This speeds up access to the files contained in these directories. If you use certain additional directories much more often than others, you can also move these directories to the front. You use a special window with a graphic representation of the directory structure for this purpose. Operation of this feature is self-explanatory.

Following a similar principle, you can also specify whether a particular file or a group of files ought to be moved to the front. By default SD favors the COM and the EXE files, for obvious reasons. Unmovable Files are files that may not be moved because they are linked to a specific cluster. Usually, these are files that have some method of copy protection. If you find files in the list before you yourself have entered any, for safety's sake, don't delete them.

Placing files in new locations

With "Show static files," the program produces a list of static files that you may not move. Among these files are the system files. The "Verify is ..." option acts as a toggle with which you can turn the verify mode on and off. If you set verify on, the work lasts longer but there will be virtually no copy errors. With verify off, SD runs faster but provides less safety.

Starting Optimization

You then start the processes with the *Optimize Disk* option (Figure 8.4). You can easily follow the copying and shifting actions on the screen if you wish, but after a while—and it can take a good hour with a full 20-Mb disk—it becomes boring. For this reason, you should only run SD when you will not need the PC for a while.

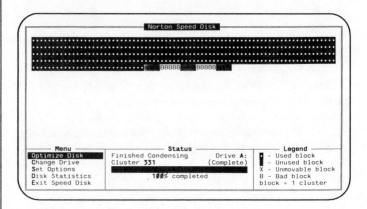

Figure 8.4: The SD (Speed Disk) program

After ending the run, SD displays an appropriate success message. If you wish, you can assure yourself of this success once again with the *Disk Statistics* menu item.

Switches

For SD, the switches allow you to set options ahead of time. The meaning of the switches corresponds to the capabilities just described. The following are the available switches:

/C   The program executes the complete optimization procedure.

/D   The program only optimizes the sequence of directories.

/Q   The program positions all used clusters at the beginning of the disk.

/U   The program only executes file optimization.

/R   The program perform no optimization—it only displays the statistics.

/S   The program also mentions the directories in the statistics.

/A   The program executes a complete optimization procedure without any user interaction.

Step 9:

Hard Disk Recovery

The worst case scenario for a PC is the unintentional formatting of a hard disk. In an instant, you can make a typing mistake and enter the disastrous FORMAT C: command. Even though all versions of MS-DOS from version 3.0 on have a security prompt, if you don't pay attention it can happen just the same. The Advanced Editions of Norton Utilities versions 4.0 and 4.5 contain a tool for recovery from this scenario, FR (Format Recover). It has a high rate of success.

This step deals with Format Recover. As you will only become acquainted with FR in a theoretical sense (who would format their hard disk just to experiment?), you will only need 15 minutes for this step.

The FR Program

Note: If you have not created a bootable system disk for the Norton Utilities, you should do so now and store at least the FR program on this floppy disk! Remember that if you unintentionally format the hard disk, you can no longer boot from it. The most practical approach is to generate a bootable floppy disk containing the most important Norton Utilities.

The basic principle of FR is the fact that little data is erased by formatting. All previously used clusters still contain stored data. Only two sources of information are in fact changed: the boot sector and the FAT (File Allocation Table). The boot sector—if you did not use the switch /S during formatting—is simply released for data storage. All entries in the FAT are reset.

Data still intact after formatting

It would be possible to just reenter all files into the FAT. However, the directory structure would be lost if you did this, and it would lead to some confusion. FR addresses this exact problem. Figure 9.1 shows FR running.

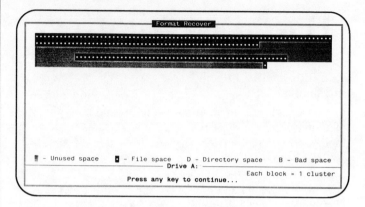

Figure 9.1: The FR (Format Recover) program

Storing System Data

FR stores important infor- mation

The program can create a file (to be precise, two files) containing the most important information about the boot sector, the FAT, and the directory structure. This data will be needed to restore the hard disk from an accidental formatting. FR stores these files so that formatting does not erase them. FR creates them automatically when you start the program like this:

```
FR C: /SAVE
```

As a safety measure, FR creates a copy of the principal file named FRECOVER.BAK. You may store this file on a floppy disk. If, during an attempt at restoring contrary to all expectations, the FR file cannot be read, copy this file to the hard disk, like so:

```
COPY FRECOVER.BAK FRECOVER.DAT
```

You can stop the program from creating the copy with the /NOBAK switch. For example,

```
FR C: /SAVE /NOBAK
```

But you should not bypass this safety feature unless your disk is very full.

You must update the FRECOVER.DAT file at regular intervals. The file only stores the state of the system at the time you run FR. This is particularly important because FR cannot use the file if its contents do not match the current state of the disk. This applies, of course, only to the changed directory structure!

For this reason, observe the following rule: Every time you delete, copy, create, or rename a directory, you should run FR with the /SAVE switch.

It is usually sufficient to run FR once a day. Otherwise, the procedure becomes complicated when you execute directory operations often.

Recovering a Formatted Disk

If the worst case scenario happens, boot the PC with the system disk containing FR. Run FR, specifying the drive letter of the formatted disk. The main menu offers four options. One of these options is to exit the program.

Save Disk Information stores the system information exactly as the /SAVE switch does. The two other options must be selected in a specific order. You must always select *Restore Disk Information* first. This option uses the stored system information. First, the program warns you that data might be destroyed or not found during recovery. You can ignore this message. The next message is more interesting. If the program finds system information, it provides the last two versions for your selection. Thus, you can either restore the last or the next-to-last state of the disk. However, if you try to use the next-to-last state, the probability is greater of encountering data that cannot be reconstructed.

The next message informs you that proceeding with the program irrevocably erases all information you may have stored on the disk since the unintentional format. You can usually ignore this message as well. If you have in fact stored

important data on the reformatted disk, you should now abort
FR and make copies of those files. The remainder of the program runs automatically.

Unformatting the Disk

In the worst possible case, either you will not have created a
file containing the system information or FR will not be able
to find the corresponding information on the formatted disk. If
so, FR will stop at the *Restore Disk Information* item and is-
sue the appropriate message. Fortunately, you will still have
the *Unformat Disk* option available.

*Success-
fully
unfor-
matting
following
SF*

This option simply reverses the formatting procedure. For the
reasons outlined above, this may result in some chaos. However, it does have a good chance of success if the disk was
formatted with the Norton Utilities SF (Safe Format) program.
If not, the data is indeed hopelessly lost.

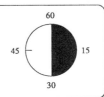

In reasonable, everyday operation, not only does the hard disk fill up with data but also the number of directories usually increases. It is not always easy to keep the upper hand when this happens. The LD (List Directories) program can help. With this program, you can display directories on the screen according to specific criteria.

This step discusses both LD and the DS (Directory Sort) program. All versions contain both programs, which have remained virtually unchanged. You will need about 30 minutes to work through this step.

The LD Program

This is the simplest Norton Utilities' program to use. You call it from the Integrator or from DOS. If you don't specify a drive letter, the program displays the current drive.

If you do not specify any other switches, the program displays a list of all directories and their subdirectories (Figure 10.1). If this list is longer than one screen page, it quickly scrolls off the screen. At the end, the program displays the total number of directories and subdirectories.

A list of the directories

Now try it this way:

```
LD C: /P
```

This time, the screen output stops when one page is full. Pressing any key brings up the next 24 lines. (Incidentally, even without the /P switch, you can stop the screen output. The program interprets the pressing of any key as a toggle to stop or start.)

```
C>ld \tc
LD-List Directories, Advanced Edition 4.50, (C) Copr 1987-88, Peter Norton

   C:\TC
   C:\TC\BGI
   C:\TC\EXAMPLES
   C:\TC\INCLUDE
   C:\TC\INCLUDE\SYS
   C:\TC\LIB

6 directories

C>
```

Figure 10.1: The LD (List Directories) program

With the /A switch, you can list all the directories on all data media in your system. This list is usually so long that you should combine the /A and /P switches.

Printing the Directory List

You can also, of course, redirect output to the printer or to a file. To do this, use the DOS redirection character (>) and specify the destination, as follows:

```
LD A: > PRN
```

or

```
LD A: > LD.LOG
```

You can get a particularly neat and clean display with the /G switch. The program displays directories graphically according to their hierarchy (Figure 10.2). You may also print this representation or redirect it to a file. If your printer is not able to print the IBM graphics characters, add the /N switch. This produces the same structure with printable characters. Here is an example:

```
LD C: /G/N > PRN
```

```
LD-List Directories, Advanced Edition 4.5Ø, (C) Copr 1987-88, Peter Norton
C:\─┬─123
     ├─123R2──────┬─ALLWAYS
     │            └─PRACTICE
     ├─123R3
     ├─ARC
     ├─BACKIT
     ├─BIN
     ├─DOC
     ├─DOS
     ├─DRIVERS
     ├─DV
     ├─ETC
     ├─FASTBACK
     ├─FASTTRAX
     ├─KERMIT
     ├─MASM────────────INCLUDE
     ├─NORTON
     ├─QEMM
     ├─TASM────────────EXAMPLES
     └─TC──────────┬─BGI
                   ├─EXAMPLES
                   ├─INCLUDE────────SYS
                   └─LIB
```

Figure 10.2: Graphic directory display using LD

Statistics

The key to effective use of statistical functions is to specify
individual directories when you run LD. For example, you can
run LD in the following way:

```
LD C:\DOS
```

And the program will display this directory together with any
subdirectories. You receive more information with the /T
switch:

```
LD C:\DOS /T
```

This command format also provides the total number of files
contained in the directory and the sum of bytes occupied by
these files. If you use this switch for an entire drive, you will
get the values for each individual directory and, at the end, for
the entire disk.

The DS Program

A quick explanation should suffice for the function of DS in
version 3.x. You run the program, specifying a sorting key
and a drive letter. The program sorts the files accordingly and
stores the new sequence on the disk.

Note: DS actually sorts the directories. Whereas all the MS-DOS tricks using filters and pipes only affect the output, DS changes the order of entries in the FAT (File Allocation Table). This order also influences how fast a file is loaded.

You create the sorting key using usually one, but up to a maximum of four, letters:

N stands for the file name.
E stands for the file-name extension.
S stands for the file size.
D stands for the file creation or modification date.
T stands for the file creation or modification time.

Specifying the sorting sequence

Normally, the program sorts in ascending order. For text-oriented specifications, this means alphabetical order—the files beginning with A come first, and so forth. If you choose to sort by size, the program lists the largest files first. Using date and time, DS sorts the files in chronological order.

The sorting direction can be reversed for any sorting key by preceding it with a minus sign. A few examples:

```
DS C: N
DS C:\DOS ES
DS C: -D-T
```

You may also specify /S as an additional switch. The program then sorts all files in all subdirectories as desired. (Unfortunately, this switch does not work in all 3.x versions.)

DS in Interactive Mode

Starting with version 4.0, DS can be run in interactive mode. In this mode, the same switches used for the old versions still apply. Now, run the DS program without switches.

The main portion of the screen is a window displaying the files and subdirectories of the current directory (Figure 10.3). DS sorts these files and subdirectories according to the criteria in force at the time.

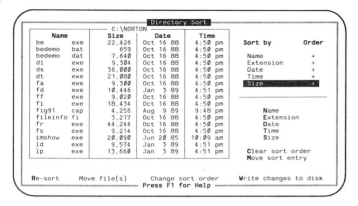

```
                        ┌─ Directory Sort ─┐
                   ┌ C:\NORTON ┐
      Name          Size       Date         Time
  be        exe      22,426   Oct 16 88     4:50 pm      Sort by          Order
  bedemo    bat         659   Oct 16 88     4:50 pm
  bedemo    dat       7,640   Oct 16 88     4:50 pm      Name               +
  di        exe       9,304   Oct 16 88     4:50 pm      Extension          +
  ds        exe      36,000   Oct 16 88     4:50 pm      Date               +
  dt        exe      21,080   Oct 16 88     4:50 pm      Time               +
  fa        exe       9,300   Oct 16 88     4:50 pm      Size               +
  fd        exe      10,446   Jan  3 89     4:51 pm
  ff        exe       9,020   Oct 16 88     4:50 pm
  fi        exe      18,434   Oct 16 88     4:50 pm      Name
  fig91     cap       4,256   Aug  9 89     9:48 pm      Extension
  fileinfo  fi        3,217   Oct 16 88     4:50 pm      Date
  fr        exe      44,244   Oct 16 88     4:50 pm      Time
  fs        exe       9,214   Oct 16 88     4:50 pm      Size
  imshow    exe      20,090   Jun 20 85    10:09 am
  ld        exe       9,574   Jan  3 89     4:51 pm      Clear sort order
  lp        exe      13,660   Jan  3 89     4:51 pm      Move sort entry

  Re-sort      Move file(s)      Change sort order      Write changes to disk
                              ── Press F1 for Help ──
```

Figure 10.3: The DS program in interactive mode

If you have not yet used DS, this sorting order is according to the sequence of entries in the FAT.

The bottom line of the window contains the options. Enter the first letter of an option to select it. You can set the sorting criteria after you have pressed **C**. After this, the program displays a marking bar in the field to the right of the file list. Select sorting criteria by entering their first letters. The criteria then appear in plain language, marked with a plus sign. You can switch between the plus sign and the minus sign by pressing + or −.

After you have entered the criteria, you can still change the order. Move the marking bar to the criterion that you wish to move. Then press **M**. Now you can move the marking bar together with its contents to the desired position. Finish the move operation by pressing Return. To delete the entire list of criteria, simply type **C**.

Changing the order of sorting criteria

Start sorting with these criteria by selecting the Re-sort option. The list of files then appears in the desired order, but the program has not yet stored this sorting order. You accomplish this by selecting *Write changes to disk.*

You can stop editing the list of criteria and return to the other options with the Esc key.

Moving Files

A seemingly insignificant feature helps you to speed up access to files you use often: you can move individual files in the sort order. You already know that a file is opened faster the higher it is located in the list of files. In the main directory, for example, the COMMAND.COM file should be located in the first position.

You move files using the same principle for moving the sorting criteria. First, bring the marking bar to the file you want to move. Then press **M**, move the bar and its contents to the desired position, and press Return.

Again, the new order will not take effect until you use the *Write changes to disk* option. In addition, you should only move individual files after sorting because global sorting, of course, also affects manually placed files.

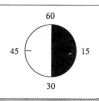

Step 11:

Finding Data

Even if you keep everything on your disk as neat as a pin, you'll sometimes be unable to find a specific file. One of the most powerful tools for searching for files is the FF (File Find) program.

Another such tool is the TS (Text Search) program. This program allows you to search the entire disk for text strings. This way, you can even find a file when you don't know its name but do know that it contains a specific phrase.

You can try out both programs in this step. Budget about 30 minutes for it.

The FF Program

You can find a file or a group of files easily with FF (Figure 11.1). The principle is similar to that of the DOS DIR command. You run the program with a switch that serves as

Finding files

```
C>ff /p
FF-File Find, Advanced Edition 4.50, (C) Copr 1987-88, Peter Norton

C:\
        io.sys          22,357 bytes  12:00 am  Fri Jul 24 87
        msdos.sys       30,128 bytes  12:00 am  Fri Jul 24 87
        123              <DIR>          2:53 pm  Sun Mar 26 89
        123R2            <DIR>          8:55 pm  Tue May 30 89
        123R3            <DIR>          6:41 pm  Sat Apr 22 89
        ARC              <DIR>          5:00 pm  Sun Mar 26 89
        BACKIT           <DIR>          8:16 am  Tue Apr  4 89
        BIN              <DIR>         10:15 am  Sun Mar 26 89
        DOC              <DIR>          6:38 pm  Sun Apr  2 89
        DOS              <DIR>         10:02 am  Sun Mar 26 89
        DRIVERS          <DIR>         10:11 am  Sun Mar 26 89
        DV               <DIR>          7:53 pm  Wed Mar 29 89
        ETC              <DIR>         10:15 am  Sun Mar 26 89
        FASTBACK         <DIR>          4:46 am  Sat Apr  1 89
        FASTTRAX         <DIR>         10:26 am  Sun Mar 26 89
        KERMIT           <DIR>          5:00 pm  Sun Mar 26 89
        MASM             <DIR>          9:44 pm  Sun Mar 26 89
        NORTON           <DIR>         10:25 am  Sun Mar 26 89
        QEMM             <DIR>          7:48 pm  Wed Mar 29 89
        TASM             <DIR>          8:16 pm  Sun Apr  9 89
Program paused; press any key to continue...
```

Figure 11.1: The FF (File Find) program

the search criterion. FF then searches through the desired drive and identifies the subdirectory containing the file you are seeking.

Naturally, you have a few additional options available. With the /A switch, the search encompasses all installed drives. The /P switch acts like the pause command in DOS; the output stops whenever it fills a screen page. You allow the output to continue by pressing any key. The /W switch lists the files found in five columns, one next to the other (as in the DOS command DIR /W).

Generating a List of Files

If you start FF without any switches, the program displays a complete list of all the directories and subdirectories on the current drive, together with all the files they contain. While this won't help you search for a specific file, it does provide a useful, neat list.

You can also send this list to the printer. Run FF like this:

```
FF > PRN
```

You can also redirect the list to a file. To do so, enter a file name instead of specifying PRN.

Statistics with FF

If you experiment, you will undoubtedly notice that the program displays the number of files found, at the end of each list. This feature allows you to produce interesting statistics. If, for example, you want to know how many BAK files (that you may want to delete) there are on the hard disk, start the program like this:

```
FF *.BAK
```

Or, you can even determine the number of text files stored for a specific project:

```
FF TEST*
```

This call produces a list of all files whose file name begins with "TEST". The number of files found will appear at the end of the list.

Wildcards

For selecting files, MS-DOS recognizes two wildcards. These are the question mark (?) and the asterisk (*). The question mark can be used within a string to take the place of one, and only one, other character. Example:

```
DIR ?OSE.TXT
```

Could result in the following:

```
HOSE.TXT
DOSE.TXT
ROSE.TXT
```

The asterisk can represent any number of characters. However, this only works at the end of a search term. For example:

```
DIR TEST*.*
```

This command could result in the following list:

```
TEST01.TXT
TEST02.TXT
TESTXX.TXT
TEST01.SIK
TEST02.SIK
TEST00.DAT
```

You may use wildcards for specifying both file names and extensions.

However, there is a shortcut available. If you are just looking for file names (including any wildcards), you may completely omit an extension—you do not have to type the final ".*".

The TS Program

Searching for text

TS (Text Search) takes one giant step beyond FF. With it, you may search files for specific phrases, among other things. An example will clarify this. Say you are looking for all files on the hard disk containing the word Intel. You then start TS like this:

```
TS C:\*.* "INTEL" /S
```

Figure 11.2 shows a possible result. TS found the term 17 times in 6 files.

```
Searching C:\ANNE\THESIS\ch4mar1.doc

Found at line 49, file offset 11,095

istory of these islands. Regrettably, little is yet known about inter-island var
iation since such a study has never been made (McCartney 1984). A common lament
is voiced by Black (1984:16), "Archaeologically, the Aleutians are known imperf
ectly. Aleut prehistory has excited the intellectual curiosity of scholars since
the 18th century, but actual archaeological investigations have been limited".

        The cultural ecological picture that emerges is one of stability and abu
ndance, where the Aleuts developed a "finely tuned" cultural ideally adapted to
the envir

Search for more (Y/N) ? Y

Searching C:\ANNE\THESIS\proposal

Search Complete

6 files found containing the text "INTEL"
17 occurrences

C>
```

Figure 11.2: The TS program finds "Intel"

Switches

The command above used an important switch: /S. This switch has the program search through all subdirectories on the disk. The /T switch has the program list only the places where it found the text instead of displaying an excerpt of the text on the screen.

Specifying the search procedure

Additional switches govern the search procedure. Normally, TS asks whether it should continue every time it finds the given phrase, but you can suppress this prompt with the /A switch. This can be useful if you need only a list of the files in which TS found the phrase. If this is what you want, call TS like this, for example:

```
TS C:\*.* "I" /S/T/A
```

The /CS switch makes the search case-sensitive. This means that the search will match only those strings with the correct upper-and lowercase letters. Consider for comparison:

```
TS C:\*.* "IBM" /CS
```

This command will find only files containing IBM in uppercase letters.

```
TS C:\.*. "ibm" /CS
```

This command would not find files containing IBM in uppercase letters but rather would find files containing, for example, the (admittedly nonsense) word "fibmaster."

Some word processors, like WordStar, alter the high bits of some characters in their documents. Using the /WS switch, you can search and TS will find matches even with altered characters. With /EBCDIC, the program can search text that uses the EBCDIC code instead of ASCII (usually, this means text coming from IBM mainframes). *Searching word-processed text*

With the /LOG switch, the program produces a record of a search action in a printable form. This record can be redirected to the printer or to a file. TS has two additional special features.

Searching the Entire Disk

With TS, you can not only search files but also investigate the names of files and directories. You can even analyze deleted data on the medium.

You can start a text search of the entire disk with the /D switch, and you can use all the switches described above with it. With /E, the program searches the erased areas of the disk. This way, you can rapidly find data for reconstruction.

Step 12:

Recovering Data

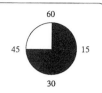

Step 12 covers the feature that made the Norton Utilities famous: data recovery. Two methods are available in all of the versions. The automatic method uses the QU (Quick UnErase) program, and the manual method uses the core NU (Norton Utility) program. As the approach of NU forms the basis for the approach of QU, we will discuss NU first.

To prepare, you should copy a few files onto your hard disk. When doing this, change the names of these files. For example, you can copy the SI.EXE program to the file TEST.TST. Do it like this:

```
COPY SI.EXE TEST.TST
```

We are going to erase this file now for test purposes and then restore it. NU's potential can be better illustrated with a large text file. If you have such a text file (bigger than 50 K) and if there is enough space on your disk, you should copy this file to the TEST.TST file.

Expect to spend 45 minutes here because this step describes various ways to recover data.

The UnErase Function in the NU Program

Before your first try at recovery, you should become acquainted briefly with the principles of data storage under DOS. You already know that the formatting process divides a device into a fixed number of tracks and sectors. A sector represents the smallest unit of storage.

Principles of data storage

On floppy disks (regardless of size and capacity), one sector can store 512 bytes. However, in most devices a file cannot occupy only a single sector because the FAT (File Allocation Table) deals with larger units.

Sectors and Clusters

For this reason, the formatting process of the device combines one or more sectors into logical units. These units are known as clusters. The following table shows the number of sectors per cluster on various media:

Device	Sectors per Cluster
5-1/4-inch floppy disks	
360 K	2
1.2 Mb	1
3-1/2-inch floppy disks	
720 K	2
1.44 Mb	1
Hard disks (some examples)	
10 Mb	2
20 Mb	4
30 Mb	4
40 Mb	4

Cluster size and capacity

Because a sector usually contains 512 bytes, the smallest possible file size on a 360 K floppy disk is 1024 bytes (1 K). For a 1.2 Mb floppy disk, it's 512 bytes; and for a 40 Mb hard disk, 2048 bytes (2 K).

If, for example, a file is 2056 bytes long, it occupies four clusters on a 1.2 Mb floppy disk. This same file occupies three clusters (!) on a 360 Kb floppy disk and two clusters on a 40 Mb disk. The space not physically used by the file but allocated because of the data organization is known as "slack." This can be identified with the FS program (see Step 13).

Directory

A direc-tory as a file

There is an entry in the root directory of the device for each file. Each entry includes the following information: name, extension, size in bytes, creation date, creation time, and start cluster. The NU program displays this structure accordingly (see Figure 12.1).

Although the names of subdirectories appear in a directory, they are listed with a size of 0.

The FAT (File Allocation Table)

All bookkeeping regarding the allocation of a device is performed using the FAT. This table contains as many entries as the device has clusters, and lists the use of each cluster. If an entry is 0, the corresponding cluster is free. The hexadecimal number F77F shows that the cluster is marked as defective and is no longer used for data storage.

Allocation of the device

If a new file is to be stored, DOS does the following:

1. Finds the first free cluster in the FAT.
2. Places the number of the first free cluster in the directory entry of the file.
3. Fills the first cluster with data. (The quantity depends on the device.)
4. Looks for the next free cluster.
5. Enters the number of this next free cluster in the entry for the first cluster.
6. Stores the next bytes of the file in this cluster.

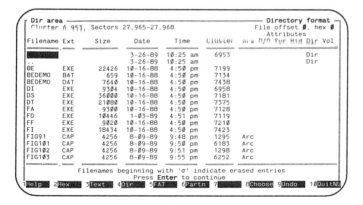

Figure 12.1: How NU represents a directory

7. As in 4.
8. As in 5.
9. As in 6, etc.

This means that DOS only rarely stores a file contiguously on a disk. The SD program (see Step 9) corrects this by storing files in consecutive clusters, using various copying processes.

Erasing a File

What actually happens when you erase a file? Previous steps mentioned that the data of a file is not, in fact, erased during deletion. Instead of that, two things happen:

- The directory entry of the file is modified.
- All entries in the FAT belonging to the deleted file are modified.

The first character of the file name is changed

The directory modification consists of the first letter of the file name being replaced by the character with an ASCII code of E5 (hexadecimal; 229 decimal). All other information is retained until the directory entry itself is overwritten. And that only happens when there are no more unused entries available for a new file.

In the FAT, all entries referring to the clusters belonging to the deleted file are set to 0. The contents of the clusters themselves are not changed. Only when another file needs free clusters for storage are these clusters formerly occupied by the deleted file overwritten. This means that it is always rather easy to recover a file if, following an unintentional deletion, you have not written anything new to the disk.

Recovering Data

If you have created a file named TEST.TST, and are certain that you have a usable copy of the file, then you can try the recovery process. First, you should view the file to be erased with the NU program. Start the program specifying the drive containing the file. If the file is not located in the root directory, specify the entire path (Figure 12.2).

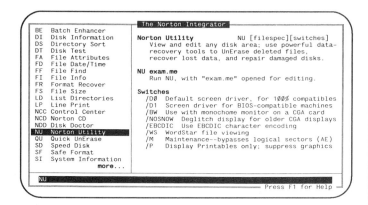

Figure 12.2: Starting NU from the Integrator

First look at the directory entry of the test file:

1. Select *Explore disk* in the main menu (Figure 12.3).
2. Select *Choose item* in Menu 1.
3. Select *File* in Menu 1.1.
4. Select *Dir area* in Menu 1.1.3.
5. Select *Edit/Display item* in Menu 1.
6. Find the entry TEST.TST in the file list.

The top left corner of the screen displays the serial number of the menu.

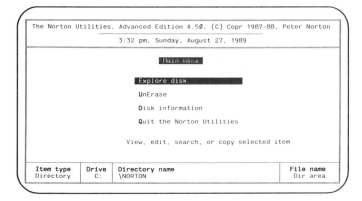

Figure 12.3: The NU main menu

You will find the information described above in the list. The name and the value for the start cluster (the "Cluster Column") are the most important pieces of information for later recovery. You should make a note of this value.

It is also interesting to see how the file appears in the FAT. You can check this if you own an Advanced Edition of the Norton Utilities. You can see the FAT representation like this:

1. Return to Menu 1 by pressing Esc.
2. Select *Choose item* in Menu 1.
3. Skip to Step 5 if the test file is located in the root directory. Otherwise, select *Change Directory* in Menu 1.1.
4. Select the root directory (the backslash symbol) in Menu 1.1.2.
5. Select *File* in Menu 1.1.
6. Select *FAT area* in Menu 1.1.3.
7. Select *Edit display item* in Menu 1.
8. Page through the FAT with the PgDn key. Look for a cluster number in the top right corner that is less than the starting cluster number of the test file you noted earlier.
9. Select the starting cluster number with the arrow keys and the Tab key.

You will see that the FAT entry for the starting cluster contains a cluster number. The cluster with this number contains a reference to the next cluster, etc.

Now you can delete the file. You already know how to do this:

```
DEL TEST.TST
```

If you list the directory with the DOS DIR command, the entry TEST.TST is not there. This is not the case if you display the directory with the NU program.

First character in the filename

Call up the directory display once again using the procedure described above. The entry differs from the previous one only in that the first letter is changed—the *T* has been replaced by the σ character. If you own an Advanced Edition, look at the FAT again. The entries for all the clusters are now 0.

Now you can reconstruct the TEST.TST file. This is also a step-by-step procedure:

1. Select *UnErase* from the main menu.
2. Select *Select erase file* from Menu 2.
3. Select *?EST.TXT* in Menu 2.2.
4. Enter the correct first letter: T.
5. Select *UnErase menu* in Menu 2.
6. In Menu 2.3, change to the right column with Tab key.
7. Select *all clusters automatically.*
8. Select the *Save erased file* item.
9. Confirm the following message by pressing any key.

With that, you have recovered the deleted file. Convince yourself of this by looking at the directory (Figure 12.4). You can also check the FAT of the device.

Recovering Data in an Emergency

In the worst case, you will have not only deleted a file but also overwritten its directory entry. You should now do this intentionally. Select another file and copy it to TEST.TST.

```
COPY NI.EXE TEST.TST
```

```
┌ Dir area ═══════════════════════════════ Directory format ┐
│ Cluster 6,953, Sectors 27,965-27,968        File offset 1,760, hex 6E0 │
│                                                    Attributes.          │
│ Filename Ext    Size      Date      Time    Cluster  Arc R/O Sys Hid Dir Vol │
│                                                                         │
│ NU       HLP    10919   10-16-88   4:50 pm   7551                       │
│ QU       EXE    18448   10-16-88   4:50 pm   7811                       │
│ READ     ME      3864   10-16-88   4:50 pm   7879                       │
│ RESEI    COM        8    5-09-89   1:08 pm   7881                       │
│ SD       EXE    67100    1-03-89   4:51 pm   7743                       │
│ SF       EXE    50896    1-03-89   4:51 pm   7776                       │
│ SI       EXE    16680    1-03-89   4:51 pm   7838                       │
│ TEST     TST    13176   10-16-88   4:50 pm   1317    Arc                │
│ TM       EXE     7504   10-16-88   4:50 pm   7821                       │
│ TS       EXE    19126   10-16-88   4:50 pm   7801                       │
│ TUT-READ ME      3537   10-16-88   4:50 pm   7920                       │
│ UD       EXE    19420   10-16-88   4:50 pm   7828                       │
│ VL       EXE    11120   10-16-88   4:50 pm   7861                       │
│ WIPEDISK EXE    13410   10-16-88   4:50 pm   7847                       │
│ WIPEFILE EXE    13176   10-16-88   4:50 pm   7854                       │
│               unused directory entry                                    │
│                                                                         │
│        Filenames beginning with 'σ' indicate erased entries            │
│                   Press Enter to continue                               │
│ 1Help  2Hex  3Text  4Dir  5FAT  6Partn  7    8Choose 9Undo  10QuitNU   │
└─────────────────────────────────────────────────────────────────────┘
```

Figure 12.4: The file list in directory format

This overwrites the directory entry of the deleted file. Unfortunately, this also overwrites the number of the starting cluster. While you still know that the data of the unintentionally deleted and overwritten file is located on the disk, you don't know where.

The NU program can help you look for and reconstruct the file. However, do not expect miracles. Clusters that have been allocated data from other files cannot revert to the original contents.

Use the following procedure to reconstruct the file:

1. Make certain that you have selected the directory in which the overwritten file was stored, or changed to this directory.
2. Select *UnErase* in the main menu.
3. Select *Select erased file* in Menu 2.
4. Select *Create file* in Menu 2.2, part 1.
5. Enter **TEST2.TST** as the filename.
6. Select *UnErase menu* in Menu 2.
7. Move to the right column of Menu 2.3 with the Tab key.
8. Select *by searching for Data* in the right column.

What does the strategy for recovering data look like now? Because you do not know where the first cluster belonging to the unintentionally overwritten file is, you must look for it using the data contained in it. This works only if you know what the file contained. When looking for Norton Utilities programs that have been overwritten, you can, for example, simply search for the word Norton that occurs in all the programs. If you search through the entire disk, sooner or later you will find a cluster containing the word. You can look at the contents of the cluster and decide whether this is indeed the correct start cluster.

9. Select *Text to search for* in Menu 2.3.2.5
10. Enter the word (or words) to search for.
11. Select *Start search* in Menu 2.3.2.5. The program automatically searches in the area of deleted data.

As soon as NU finds a cluster containing the text you are looking for, you get a screen message that you must confirm by pressing any key. Then, you get Menu 2.3.2.5.2.

12.   Select *Display/Edit cluster(s)* in Menu 2.3.2.5.2.

You can now see the contents and decide whether this is the correct starting cluster. You can page through the contents with the cursor keys and the PgUp and PgDn keys. You complete checking the cluster contents by pressing Return.

13.   If this is the correct cluster, select *Add cluster(s) to file* and proceed with Step 14a. If this is not the correct cluster, select *Skip cluster(s)* and proceed with step 14b.

14a. End the data search by pressing the Esc key.
14b. Select *Continue Search* in Menu 2.3.2.5 and go to step 12.
15.   Select *Next probable cluster* in Menu 2.3.
16.   If this next cluster is the correct one, select Add cluster(s) to file and go to step 17a. If this is not the next correct cluster, select *Skip cluster(s)* and proceed with step 17b.
17a. Continue with step 15. Once you have completely or at least satisfactorily reconstructed the file by looking for and adding the clusters, select *Save Erased File* in the left column of Menu 2.3 and then select *Leave UnErase*. You have recovered the overwritten file.
17b. If, in spite of a complete search, you do not find any clusters that fit the overwritten file, the recovery attempt has failed. You can exit Menu 2.3 by pressing the Esc key.

The QU Program

Data recovery with the QU (Quick UnErase) program is much simpler. You start the program using the name of the directory containing the deleted file as a switch.

*Quick
data
recovery*

QU then looks in the directory for deleted files, specifies how many deleted files it has found, and provides the found files for recovery. You need only confirm that you want to recover the displayed file and then specify the first letter of the file name. The rest of the procedure is automatic (see Figure 12.5).

QU even finds different versions of files having the same name. Here, you must try to determine which file you meant, using the information regarding the file size and creation date or time.

However, QU can only recover files when you have not yet overwritten the directory entry and the cluster entries in the FAT have not yet been used in some other way. In any other case, QU is powerless.

Recovering several files

You can start QU specifying a precise file name or a file name containing wildcards. If QU then finds a file with a name corresponding to the specified name, except for a first letter, this first letter is automatically set. For example:

```
QU \TOOLS\SI.EXE
```

This recovers the file SI.EXE automatically.

```
QU \TOOLS\??.EXE
```

This command recovers all EXE files having a file name consisting of two characters.

```
C>qu c:/norton
QU-Quick UnErase, Advanced Edition 4.50, (C) Copr 1987-88, Peter Norton

Directory of C:\NORTON
    Erased file specification: *.*
    Number of erased files: 1
    Number that can be Quick-UnErased: 1

    Erased files lose the first character of their names.
    After selecting each file to Quick-UnErase, you will be
    asked to supply the missing character.

    ?est.tst        42,972 bytes      4:51 pm  Tue Jan  3 89
    Quick-UnErase this file (Y/N) ?
```

Figure 12.5: The result of a QU (Quick UnErase) run

Because, here, QU does not know which file had which name, it assigns code letters alphabetically. For example, QU could create the following file lists after a run:

```
AA.EXE
AB.EXE
AC.EXE
AD.EXE
```

Following the same principle, the program recovers all erased files of a directory if you specified automatic recovery with the /A switch. Then, QU starts with file names consisting of one character:

```
A.BAT
B.EXE
C.DAT
D.COM
```

Identifying Files

Following such an automatic run, unfortunately, you must analyze each individual file to be able to give it the proper file name.

Step 13:

Editing Your Files

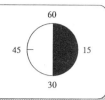

Step 13 covers various capabilities for editing files. The FA
(File Attributes) and FS (File Size) programs come with all
versions. Version 4.0 also contains FI (File Info). You will not
find the FD (File Date/Time) program until version 4.5. You
may try out all four programs on existing files without danger.
You don't have to worry about unintentional damage. This
step should take about 30 minutes.

The FA Program

DOS assigns a maximum of four attributes to each file. Of
these four, you can change two with the DOS ATTRIB command (provided in MS-DOS 3.x and later). Each of the following attributes is either valid or invalid for a file:

*A maxi-
mum of
four
attributes*

Archive   If the archive bit is set, the file will be included
               in the next backup. If this bit is not set, the file
               will be ignored during backup.

Hidden   If the hidden attribute is set, the file does not
               appear with the DOS DIR command.

Read-only   If the read-only attribute is set, you may only
               read the file, not modify it.

System   If the system attribute is set, DOS treats the file
               as a system file. The DOS DIR command does
               not display the file and the SYS command cop-
               ies the file to a data medium.

With FA, you can search for and display files having a specific attribute, and only that attribute. You can also change one
or more attributes for a specified group of files.

Displaying Attributes

When starting FA to list files, you must specify the attributes of the group of files. If you do not specify a file description, FA assumes that you want to see all the files ("*.*"). Figure 13.1 shows a sample FA run.

The second switch determines the attribute you wish to use for the listing:

/A	Archive
/HID	Hidden
/R	Read-only
/SYS	System

You may also use more than one attribute as criteria for the listing. In these cases, the program only displays those files having all specified attributes set.

Four additional switches are possible. These mainly have to do with the search range and screen display:

/P   The program stops the output when a screen page is full. You continue display by pressing any key.

/S   The program also searches all subdirectories of the current directory.

```
C>fa c:\ /r
FA-File Attributes, Advanced Edition 4.50, (C) Copr 1987-88, Peter Norton

C:\
    io.sys              Read-only Hidden System
    msdos.sys           Read-only Hidden System

    2 files shown
    0 files changed

C>
```

Figure 13.1: The FA program

/T The program displays not only the individual file names but also the total number of files in question.

/U The program displays all files having one or more of the attributes set. Files with no attributes set are ignored.

Setting and Clearing Attributes

You can also set or clear all attributes with FA. The most radical switch is named /CLEAR. With this switch, the program resets all attributes of the selected files. With other switches, you can proceed in a selective fashion.

You set an attribute by appending a plus sign to the corresponding switch. You clear the attribute with a minus sign. So, for instance, you could make all BAT files invisible like this:

```
FA C:\*.bat /HID+ /S
```

or, you could specify that all BAK files were to be ignored during the next total backup like this:

```
FA C:\*.BAK /A- /S
```

If you want to copy the AUTOEXEC and the CONFIG files from your system disk to all future boot disks, simply make these system files:

Tricks with FA

```
FA AUTOEXEC.BAT /S+
FA CONFIG.SYS /S+
```

The FS Program

The FS (File Size) program is particularly useful before you copy several files. It adds the sizes of selected files. The program can also determine whether there is enough space for these files on a given destination drive.

Using FS is very simple. You specify the file or the group of files as switches (you may use all wildcards). If necessary, you can also specify the destination drive and an optional

Total size of groups of files

switch. FS displays the list and the sum of the sizes. In the following example, the program looks at all text files in the C:\TEXT directory. It determines whether there is enough space on the floppy disk in the A: drive for the selected files.

```
FS C:\TEXT\*.TXT A:
```

You can see the results in Figure 13.2. As you can also see, the program displays the total capacity of the source drive. The display of the amount of slack (see Step 12) is particularly interesting.

You can also use the well-known /P, /S, and /T switches. Specifying /T is useful when you only want to know the sum and do not need a list of files.

```
qu.exe            18,448 bytes
read.me            3,864 bytes
reset.com              8 bytes
sd.exe            67,100 bytes
sf.exe            50,896 bytes
si.exe            16,680 bytes
fig125.cap         4,256 bytes
tm.exe             7,504 bytes
ts.exe            19,126 bytes
tut-read.me        3,537 bytes
ud.exe            19,420 bytes
vl.exe            11,120 bytes
wipedisk.exe      13,410 bytes
wipefile.exe      13,176 bytes
fig124.cap         4,256 bytes
fig131.cap         4,256 bytes

1,139,685 total bytes in 63 files
1,222,656 bytes disk space occupied, 6% slack

Drive usage
33,409,024 bytes available on drive C:
6,909,952 bytes unused on drive C:, 21% unused

C>
```

Figure 13.2: The FS (File Size) program

The FD Program

*Changing
the date
and time
stamp*

This program first became available with version 4.5. With FD (File Date/Time), you can change the date and time stamps of one or more files. Specify the file names or the group of files (you may use all wildcards) and either /D or /T or both.

With /D, the program sets the creation date to the current system date. With /T, it sets the creation time to the current system time.

```
FD C:\*.LOG /D/S
```

This command changes the creation date of all LOG files in all subdirectories to the current system date.

```
FD C:\TEXT\*.TXT T00:00:00
```

This command stamps all TXT files in the specified directory with the specified time.

The FI Program

This program first became available with version 4.0. It can be used as a substitute for the DOS DIR command. The main difference is that this program can list files of a group extending through all the directories of a data medium.

Substitute for the DOS DIR command

You can also provide every file with explanatory comments. Users who have trouble managing with the cryptic abbreviations possible with the eight letters of a filename will especially like this feature. Figure 13.3 shows a sample FI run.

```
C>fi c:\*.log /s/p
FI-File Info, Advanced Edition 4.50, (C) Copr 1987-88, Peter Norton

  Directory of C:\NORTON

ndd      log      2,616    8-17-89    9:13p  \*.log
ndd1     log      2,618    8-17-89    9:17p  \*.log

2 files found    6,901,760 bytes free

C>
```

Figure 13.3: The FI (File Info) program

Listing a File

For displaying lists of files, you use FI just like the DOS DIR command. You can specify a directory name and use wildcards.

You can have the output stop every time a screen page is filled with the /P switch.

With the /S switch, you direct the program to consider all sub-directories. If you want to see all the LOG files on your hard disk, enter the following:

```
FI C:\*.LOG /S/P
```

Editing Comments

You may assign comments to a file. To do this, specify the appropriate text as a switch. The comments are stored in a file called FILEINFO.F1. Try assigning a comment to this very file.

```
FI FILEINFO.FI The collected comments
```

The file FILEINFO.FI gets the comment "The collected comments". Of course, you can also assign a single comment to a group of files. For example:

```
FI C:\*.LOG This is a log file /S
```

Miscellaneous Switches

The following switches make working with FI easier.

/C   The program only lists files that are assigned comments.

/D   FI deletes all comments assigned to the selected files.

/E   You can assign or change comments using the built-in editor.

/L   FI completely displays comments with more than 35 characters. (Without this switch, the program truncates long comments after the 35th character.)

/N   When this is used with the /E switch, FI adapts the output to non-ANSI terminals.

/PACK   The program compresses the file FILEINFO.FI (that contains all of the comments of the files in one directory) so that it consumes less space on the device.

Step 14:

Directory Recovery

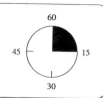

You have a big enough problem when you erase individual files. However, when you also erase the subdirectories containing these files, there are few chances of recovering the data. This step covers the UD (UnRemove Directory) program used to recover unintentionally deleted directories.

You should try out the effect of UD on an example. Budget about 15 minutes for this.

The UD program

Create a new directory named UNREMOVE on your hard disk. Copy a few files to this directory. As a precaution, check the results with the DOS DIR command.

Delete and recover the directory

You will soon delete this example directory and recover it again. You already know that you can only delete a directory if it is empty. For this reason, you must first delete all the files in the UNREMOVE directory. (If you are working with the GEM user interface, you can delete an entire directory together with its contents with a single command, in contrast to DOS.)

For this reason, change to the new UNREMOVE directory. Delete all files there:

```
DEL *.*
```

Now the directory is empty and can be deleted itself. Check this state with the DOS DIR command. Then change to the parent directory and delete the UNREMOVE directory with the following command:

```
RD UNREMOVE
```

Starting UD

There are two methods for starting UD. You can either start the program without switches or by specifying the name of the unintentionally deleted directory.

You know from Step 12 that deleting a file or directory only changes the first letter of its name. This signifies that the space occupied by this file or directory is available.

If you specify a name for the directory to be recovered and the program finds a deleted directory matching this input except for the first letter the program completes the found name correctly.

If you do not specify any switches, UD investigates the current directory and offers any deleted directories it finds for recovery. If a directory you deleted unintentionally is there, you need only enter the correct first letter (Figure 14.1).

Reconstructing Files

The UD program only restores the directory itself. You must also reconstruct the files contained in this directory with the QU (Quick UnErase) program. To do this, proceed as described in Step 12.

```
C>ud unremove.*
UD-UnRemove Directory, Advanced Edition 4.50, (C) Copr 1987-88, Peter Norton

Directory of C:\NORTON
    Removed directory specification: UNREMOVE.*
    Number of removed directories: 1
    Number that can be UnRemoved: 1

    ?NREMOVE          <DIR>        4:38 pm  Sun Aug 27 89
Enter the first character of the filename: U

    ?d.exe           67,100 bytes  4:51 pm  Tue Jan  3 89
    ?f.exe           50,896 bytes  4:51 pm  Tue Jan  3 89
    ?i.exe           16,680 bytes  4:51 pm  Tue Jan  3 89

Files included in C:\NORTON\UNREMOVE

'.UNREMOVE' UnRemoved

C>
C>
C>
C>
C>
```

Figure 14.1: The UD (UnRemove Directory) program

Step 15:

Changing Directories

The NCD (Norton Change Directory) program included in the Norton Utilities since version 4.0 is very popular, particularly among PC tyros. There is good reason for this. NCD manages the entire directory structure of a data medium without the user having to be concerned with the various levels.

This step shows you how to best put NCD to use. You will need about 15 minutes to study this step.

The NCD Program

When working with the NCD program, you must differentiate between two different uses:

- NCD as a substitute for the DOS CD command;
- NCD as a user interface for directory management.

Initially, let's consider the first approach. First, make sure that you have created a path to the directory containing the Norton Utilities. To do this, insert the following line in the AUTOEXEC.BAT file:

Creating a path

```
PATH C:\NORTON
```

or specify the name of the directory containing the Norton Utilities. If your AUTOEXEC file already contains a PATH command, you need only append the directory name, as in this example:

```
PATH C:\DOS;C:\TEXT;C:\NORTON
```

This path specification is a prerequisite allowing you to call the NCD program from every subdirectory. When you call NCD for the first time, the program creates a special file named TREEINFO.NCD in the main directory. This file contains all of the information regarding the directory structure of the disk.

Update TREE- INFO regularly

You can keep the program from creating TREEINFO.NCD by starting NCD with the /N switch. Unfortunately, NCD updates TREEINFO.NCD only when you change the directory structure using the NCD program. If you make changes with one of the DOS commands, TREEINFO.NCD is not brought up to date. You must start NCD with the /R switch to record the most recent changes in TREEINFO.NCD. After this, NCD again operates with correct data.

NCD as a Substitute for CD

You should completely refrain from using the DOS commands CD (Change Directory), MD (Make Directory) and RD (Remove Directory). This is because working with the corresponding NCD options is substantially easier and much quicker.

When creating and deleting directories, the NCD program acts just like the corresponding DOS commands. For example:

```
NCD MD \NORTON\TEXT
```

This command creates the TEXT subdirectory in the NORTON directory.

```
NCD RD \NORTON\TEXT
```

This command deletes this subdirectory again, as long as there are no files in this subdirectory.

Changing from directory to directory is more interesting. For this, NCD provides two advantages.

* You only need to specify the directory name and not the entire path. For example, entering **NCD TEST** changes to the directory C:\NORTON\TEST, independently of what the current directory is when you call the program.

- You do not need to specify the entire directory name because NCD automatically completes the rest. In fact, if you only specify the first letter, NCD changes to the first directory in the hierarchy with a name that starts with this letter. If you repeat the command, NCD looks for the next such directory, and so forth. (With DOS, you can repeat the last command with the F3 key.)

Using NCD interactively

You can run NCD directly from DOS or by way of the Integrator. When running the program, you need not specify switches, but you can use /N or /R, as already mentioned.

The program displays the entire directory structure of the disk in a graphic form (Figure 15.1). You can move within this directory tree with the cursor keys. With the left and right arrow keys, you move within one level of the hierarchy. You change between levels with the up and down arrows. As usual, you can also use the PgDn and PgUp keys for greater movement. The Home key moves you to the main directory of the disk (topmost entry or root). With End, you move to the last, or bottom, entry in the directory tree.

Graphic directory structure

The program uses highlighted letters to display the initial directory, that is, the directory that is current when you call

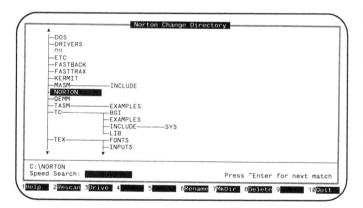

Figure 15.1: The NCD program in version 4.0

NCD. Use the marking bar to indicate the directory to change to. You change directories by pressing the Return key. However, the change does not take effect until you exit NCD with Esc or F10.

The bottom area of the NCD screen displays the name of the directory highlighted by the marking bar, including its entire path specification. This area also contains the names of the four possible commands. You can select one of these commands using the highlighted letter. You can create, delete and rename a directory. The *Home directory* command always returns you to the directory from which you called NCD.

NCD in Version 4.5

NCD with speed search

Version 4.5 contains a speed search feature that works just like the speed search in the Norton Integrator. You can now also quickly select the options with function keys. You can change the drive used to display the directory tree by pressing F3. The TREEINFO.NCD file can also be updated from inside the program. The *Lines* option is new. With it, you can increase the number of lines displayed on the screen when using EGA or VGA graphics. Do this to display more directory entries and make the display easier to understand.

Step 16:

Analyzing Your Disks

Steps 16, 17, and 18 again deal with the core program of the Norton Utilities. You became acquainted with NU as a data recovery tool in Step 12. In the next three steps, you will learn that NU can also accomplish a series of tasks you are already familiar with. Among these tasks are the analysis and editing of a disk.

NU provides more flexibility than the special programs for these activities. Since you use programs such as DT, VL, and WipeDisk in the everyday world of PCs, the following three steps only briefly discuss the special capabilities of NU.

NU starts with disk analysis. Beginning with version 3.0, it contains all the necessary commands and menu items. The versions differ from one another in varying degrees. Where these differences are important for your work, various versions will be discussed separately. Each procedure for version 3.0 is specified as a series of steps. You should expect to spend about 30 minutes.

Floppy Disk Data

Start the NU program. If you want to investigate a disk other than the one that contains the Norton Utilities, specify the drive letter as a switch.

The screen display may be difficult to read. The differences between highlighted and normal characters may not be clear, or there may be some other problems. If any of these problems occur, try starting NU with the following switches, one after another:

Changing the screen display

/D1　Use this switch if your graphics adapter is not IBM-compatible.

/D2	Use this switch if your system is running without ANSI.SYS or if you cannot use ANSI.SYS as the screen driver.
/B7/F0	Use these switches if you wish to change the background and foreground colors. Use the desired color code in each case.
/BW	Use this switch if you operate a monochrome screen on a color graphics adapter (CGA, EGA, or VGA).

From the main menu (Figure 16.1), select the *Disk Information* item. Menu 3 contains the options for analyzing the disk.

First try the *Technical Information* option.

Technical Information

Information regarding the disk

The following screen provides you with the most important information on the type and assignment of the selected disk. This data is identical to what you get with the DI program. However, it is in a different form here. The program displays the total capacity, the free-memory capacity and the logical dimensions of the disk. From this data, you can learn how many logical disks your hard disk drive contains, how many

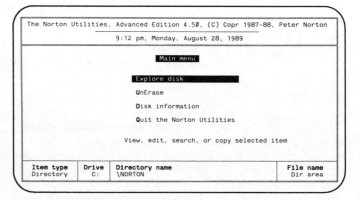

Figure 16.1: The NU main menu

clusters the current partition has, and so forth. This information is not very important for later work.

Disk Map

Return to Menu 3 by pressing any key. There, select the *Map disk usage* option. This way, you receive a true-to-scale representation of the usage of the disk (Figure 16.2). The scale is based on the total capacity of the disk. With a 20-Mb disk, for example, a small box represents 21 clusters. Each little box displays the primary makeup of the corresponding area. Black squares symbolize assigned areas, hatched boxes depict free areas. A blinking *B* represents a cluster containing bad sectors.

Using this map, you can determine how large the defective areas are. You can also see how severely the individual files are fragmented. An optimal disk or one that the SD program (see Step 8) has just optimized has the used clusters in the upper area and the free clusters in the lower area. Alternating free and used areas on the disk are a sign of an improperly managed disk.

Infor-mation from the disk map

Analysis Using Norton Utility 3.x

You get the same information with the NU program of version 3.x using the following procedure:

1. Start the NU program from DOS.
2. Press the F2 key or **2** to select *Explore Disk Information.*
3. Press the F2 key or **2** to select *Display Disk Technical Information.*
4. Exit Menu 2.2 by pressing any key.
5. Press the F3 key or **3** to select *Map Space Usage of Entire Disk.*

Directory Information

The facilities for observing and changing directory files differ from version to version. NU 3.x allows you to obtain information regarding individual directory entries.

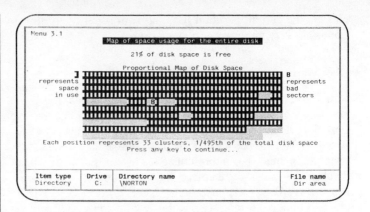

```
Menu 3.1
                    Map of space usage for the entire disk
                        21% of disk space is free
                      Proportional Map of Disk Space
            ]  ▓▓▓▓▓▓▓▓▓▓▓▓▓▓▓▓▓▓▓▓▓▓▓▓▓▓▓▓▓▓▓▓▓▓▓▓  B
     represents ▓▓▓▓▓▓▓▓▓▓▓▓▓▓▓▓▓▓▓▓▓▓▓▓▓▓▓▓▓▓▓▓▓▓▓  represents
          space ▓▓▓▓▓▓▓▓▓▓▓▓▓▓▓▓▓▓▓▓▓▓▓▓▓▓▓▓▓▓▓▓     bad
        in use  ▓▓▓▓▓▓▓▓▓▓▓▓▓     ▓▓▓ B ▓▓▓▓▓▓▓▓▓▓▓  sectors
                ▓▓▓▓▓▓▓▓▓▓▓▓▓▓▓▓▓▓▓▓▓▓▓▓▓▓▓▓▓▓▓▓▓▓▓
                ▓▓▓▓▓▓▓▓▓▓▓▓▓▓▓▓▓▓▓▓▓▓▓▓   ▓▓▓▓▓▓▓▓
                ▓▓▓▓▓▓▓▓▓▓▓▓▓▓▓▓▓▓▓▓▓▓▓▓▓▓▓▓▓▓▓▓▓▓
     Each position represents 33 clusters, 1/495th of the total disk space
                      Press any key to continue...

  Item type    Drive   Directory name                         File name
  Directory      C:    \NORTON                                Dir area
```

Figure 16.2: The illustration of disk assignment in NU

1. Start the NU program from DOS.
2. Press the F1 key or **1** to select *Change Selection.*
3. Press the F3 or **3** to select *Select file.*
4. Select *.(this dir)* in the file list.
5. Press the F2 or **2** to select *Explore the Disk Information.*
6. Press the F4 key or **4** to select *Display Information about Selected Item.*
7. Page though the directory entries with the cursor keys.
8. Return to the main menu by pressing the Esc key twice.

For each entry, the program specifies the name of the file represented by the entry, the attributes, the creation date, and creation time. It also shows the starting cluster and the size of the file.

Versions 4.0 and 4.5 also contain this table of the directory entries. Follow this route to that information:

1. Select *Explore Disk* in the main menu.
2. Select *Choose Item* in Menu 1.
3. Select *File* in Menu 1.1.
4. Select any file in Menu 1.1.3.
5. Select *Information on item* in Menu 1.

Use the cursor keys to see other entries (see Figure 16.3).

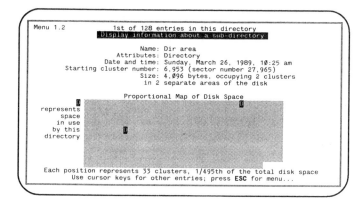

Figure 16.3: NU supplies information about a directory entry

You can get a different form of the directory representation using a procedure that is almost identical. In Menu 1, you need only select *Edit/Display Item*. This directory representation leans heavily on the one used by DOS (see Figure 16.4). You get the file name, the extension, the size, creation date and time, the starting cluster, and the attributes.

You may page through this list with the up and down arrows and the PgDn, PgUp, Home and End keys. Deleted entries are identified by a σ replacing the first character.

Key functions

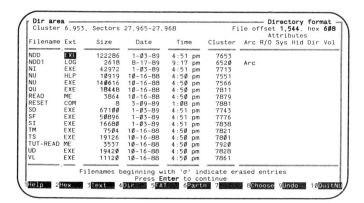

Figure 16.4: Directory entries in the NU directory format

You can switch between the two other directory forms with the F2 and F3 function keys, but the text mode (F3) is not suitable for viewing directories. You can, however, manipulate the directory entries in hex mode. You will learn how to do this in Step 17.

Working on a Directory with the Advanced Edition

Manipulating directory entries

The Advanced Editions also offer the capability of manipulating directory entries. You do this directly in the representation of the directory format.

You can move a marking bar from column to column and from line to line with the arrow keys, the Tab key, and the PgDn, PgUp, Home, and End keys. Then you can edit the entry you have marked.

To change file names and extensions, you must delete the character to be changed with the Del key and then enter the new character in this position. Be careful using the spacebar! This key does not enter a blank but rather creates a separation. This means that the characters following a blank inserted in this manner do not appear later in the name or the extension. It is best to delete all the characters in a name or an extension and then to retype the entire entry.

Conclude every change with the Return key. As long as you do not exit from the directory representation, the changes are temporary. You can select a changed field and revert to the initial setting by pressing the F9 key. Incidentally, you can recognize changed fields by the bright letters.

Validity check

The program automatically corrects impossible values if you change the creation date and time. For example, if you want to enter 35 May, the program will make this 31 May. The program likewise does not recognize a 13th month. It only accepts values between 80 and 99 for the year. The program also corrects hours greater than 23 and minutes greater than 59.

There is also a similar validity check for the specification of the starting cluster. NU automatically sets all entries greater than the total number of clusters to this maximum value.

Note! If you assign several entries to the same starting cluster, the result will be chaos on your disk. Extensive data loss is a certainty! For this reason, manipulate this value only in the most extreme emergency!

For the attributes, you switch between the two possible states in each case using the space bar.

As a rule, you will use the directory editor only to restore directories and files, to rename them, or to change their creation dates and times.

Step 17:

Editing Data Directly

Step 17 deals with changing data directly where it is stored. You use the menu item *Edit/Display Item* in the NU program for this purpose. However, this type of work on a sector basis is a task only for specialists who are confident of avoiding all unintentional data loss. You will need about 15 minutes for this step.

The Hex editor

To edit data directly on the disk, you must first run NU. From the main menu, select *Explore Disk*. You will then continue in Menu 1.

To specify the file to be changed, first select *Choose Item*. You can change to another drive or another directory, if necessary, in Menu 1.1. Select a file from the current directory with the *File* menu item (Figure 17.1).

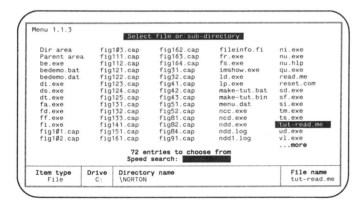

Figure 17.1: The file lists in Menu 1.1.3 of NU

Speed searching in NU

You already know how to make this type of selection. Move the marking bar to the desired file name with the arrow keys or the PgDn, PgUp, Home, or End keys. Confirm the selection with the Return key. Of course, you can also use the convenient speed-search method. This method is best for file lists that do not fit on one screen page. Look for a file that is not important (the file TUTORIAL.NTS included with the Norton package, for example), or create such a file yourself—the contents make no difference.

Then switch to *Edit/Display Item* in Menu 1. There are now two possibilities. If you have selected a pure text file, the contents of the file appear in text format (Figure 17.2). In this mode, you can view the contents of the file but you cannot change it. However, you can still find out a lot of valuable information regarding the selected file.

The top line of the screen displays the file name. Beneath this, you will find information regarding the starting and ending clusters occupied by this file or the numbers of the sectors combined to form these clusters. The top right corner shows, as an orientation aid, your position in the file relative to the beginning.

The hexa-decimal system

You cannot edit the individual bytes until you are in the hex format. Hex stands for hexadecimal, or the hexadecimal system.

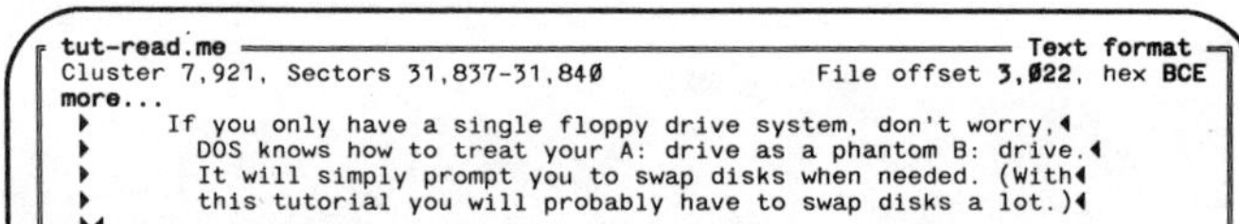

Figure 17.2: A file displayed in text format by NU

This is a base 16 number system, and it is particularly well suited to represent bytes. One byte can represent decimal values from 0 to 255 and hexadecimal values from 0 to FF. So all the numbers that can be represented by one byte can be represented with a two-digit hexadecimal number. In the hexadecimal system, you count 1, 2, 3, 4, 5, 6, 7, 8, 9, A, B, C, D, E, F. In this system, A corresponds to the decimal number 10, B corresponds to 11, and F corresponds to 15. Using these 255 hex numbers you can also represent the 255 characters of the expanded ASCII character set.

Now look at the file you just selected in hex format (see Figure 17.3). The program divides the screen vertically into two sections. On the left, you see 22 lines of six columns each. The contents of these lines are hex numbers. On the right, you see 22 lines of 24 characters each in text format.

A block cursor blinks on the left side. You can control this cursor with the usual keys. You make changes by simply overwriting the file. Since this area contains hex numbers, you may only enter letters from A to F and numerals. (You may use either upper- or lowercase letters.)

Of course, you don't keep hex numbers in your head. You also do not know the ASCII codes for important characters by heart. Luckily, you don't need to. The right section displays

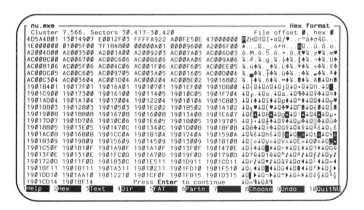

Figure 17.3: A file displayed in hex format by NU

the hex numbers as ASCII characters. This means that every two characters on the left side represent one hex number. One ASCII character on the right side corresponds to every two characters on the left side. Fortunately, each area has its own cursor. These cursors move in parallel with each other. If you move the cursor on the left side one line downward, the (un-blinking) cursor on the right side follows this movement.

Switching between hex and ASCII

You can also have the blinking cursor in the ASCII area. Push the Tab key. Now, the cursor in the ASCII area controls the cursor in the hex area. You can still only edit in the area containing the blinking cursor. However, changes occur in both areas in parallel.

If, for example, in the hex area you change the number 4E to the number 57, the ASCII character N becomes a W. On the other hand, if you replace the N with a W in the ASCII area, the corresponding hex number will be changed.

The changes are only temporary at first

The program highlights all changes to a file using bold characters. Every change is temporary until you exit the editor. Before this, you can reset every change by moving to a changed hex number or ASCII character (changed characters will be bright) and pressing the F9 key.

Now change some data in your experimentation file. You will see that in this way you can change, for example, the English menu designations to German. You can also do a lot more.

However, you must observe one basic rule under all circumstances. If you change text in an executable file (with an extension of EXE or COM, or possibly OVL or something similar), then this text must have exactly the same length as the original text. If it is longer, you may overwrite program code. You can pad shorter text with blanks.

After experimenting, exit the editor with the Esc key. Then in Menu 1.3, you must decide how you are going to treat the changes. You may write the changes to the hard disk (*Write the changed data*). You may also check the changes again (*Review the changed data*) or leave the file in its original state (*Discard the changes*).

If you are not completely certain that your changes were correct, you should check them again. Only when you are absolutely convinced should you write the changes to the disk.

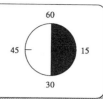

Step 18:

Special Features

A few advanced applications are possible using the NU core program. However, these applications involve a very serious invasion of the system. Step 18 deals with this type of invasion. You should only work through this step when you are confident of avoiding unintentional data loss. As some experimentation is necessary for the advanced applications, you should take about 30 minutes for this step.

The Settings

It is a little-known fact that some settings can be made after you have already started NU. Combinations using Alt and a function key have the effects listed below:

Alt-F1   This key combination switches between mono-chrome and color representation.

Alt-F2   You switch to Print mode with this command. In this mode, the program only displays printable characters.

Alt-F3   This command changes the color of the letters. Every time you use it, the program selects the next color code, ranging from 0 to 15.

Alt-F4   This command changes the background color. Every time you use it, the program selects the next color code, ranging from 0 to 15.

Alt-F5   Using this key combination, you can switch the output from ASCII to EBCDIC and back.

Alt-F6   With this command, you produce a "WordStar" representation, ignoring special characters.

Editing Clusters and Sectors

Up to now, as far as you know, you have only manipulated files with NU. This is because NU treats files as a collection of the clusters occupied by these files. Even the work done on directories affects only specific sectors.

You can easily check this. Let's assume that you want to analyze the boot sector of a floppy disk. This area is not designated anywhere as a file. You must appropriate it as a sector. Before you do this, you should format a floppy disk with DOS. This floppy disk should only contain data that you no longer need.

Note! Do not perform the following experiments on your hard disk under any circumstances! You must use a floppy disk containing no important data. All of these experiments can result in the complete destruction of the stored data. Data destroyed in the following manipulations cannot be constructed with any utility.

Start the NU program if you have not already done so. Select *Explore disk* in the main menu and *Choose Item* in Menu 1. In Menu 1.1, first select *Change Drive*. Change to the drive containing your experimentation floppy disk. Then, select *Sector*.

In the following screen, NU specifies which sector numbers are valid for the selected disk. In addition, you'll find a list of the sector allocations. The program also specifies here that the boot sector is number 0 (this is the case for every disk).

Reading format information

This area contains the format information; it also contains the other data required by DOS for reading the disk. You can check this if you switch to the editor with *Edit/Display Item* (Figure 18.1). There, you will immediately find in the first few bytes a notice regarding the DOS version used during formatting.

This entry might read "MSDOS3.3" or "PCDOS3.0", for example. Overwrite it with any text you like as long as it is the same length. "TESTCASE" usually fits exactly. Now, exit the editor. On the next screen, you can specify whether the change is

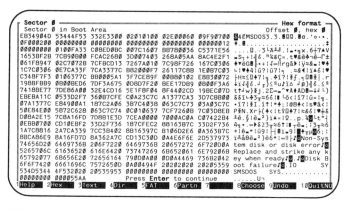

Figure 18.1: Boot sector of a floppy disk shown with NU

to be written onto the disk. Select *Write the changed data* there. As the program recognizes that this change is a serious intervention in sector 0, you will receive an additional warning on the screen. You may ignore this warning and confirm that you want to make the change.

You may check the changes to the boot sector with the DI program, which displays the DOS version in the form stored on the floppy disk (Figure 18.2). The change you made was rather harmless. With the same methods, you could also change some of the floppy disk's technical data. For example,

```
C>di a:
DI-Disk Information, Advanced Edition 4.50, (C) Copr 1987-88, Peter Norton

   Information from DOS          Drive A:        Information from the boot record
-----------------------------------------------------------------------------------
                          system id              'TESTCASE'
                          media descriptor (hex)       F9
              0           drive number
            512           bytes per sector            512
              1           sectors per cluster           1
              2           number of FATs                2
            224           root directory entries      224
              7           sectors per FAT               7
          2,371           number of clusters
                          number of sectors         2,400
              1           offset to FAT                 1
             15           offset to directory
             29           offset to data
                          sectors per track            15
                          sides                         2
                          hidden sectors                0

C>
```

Figure 18.2: DI displays the change to the boot sector

113

you could artificially reduce its capacity by filling portions of
the FAT with a value of FF (hexadecimal).

Copying Files

To a certain extent, the program hides the ability to copy files.
This is very advisable—as has already been mentioned several times.

1. Start the NU program.
2. Select *Explore disk* in the main menu.
3. Confirm *Choose Item* in Menu 1.
4. Select *File* in Menu 1.1.
5. Select the desired file from the list of files.
6. Select *Write item to disk* in Menu 1.
7. Select *File mode*.
8. Select the drive to which you will write.
9. Specify a file name for the copy.
10. Confirm the message that the file is to be written.

Incidentally, you can also write data not available in the form
of a file (e.g., the contents of the boot sector) to a file in this
manner. You can also copy individual sectors and clusters
(Figure 18.3).

Making a
bit copy

With a little manual work, you can, for example, make an exact bit copy of the entire floppy disk. In this manner, you

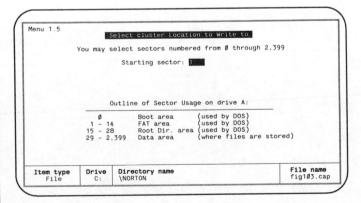

Figure 18.3: Copying sectors exactly with NU

could analyze and change even complicated copy-protection mechanisms. This is because a sector-by-sector copy of a floppy disk precisely copies even all hidden, non-system compatible and apparently damaged areas.

Editing Partitions

Only the owners of Advanced Editions are able to analyze and change the partition table of a hard disk. Do not experiment with this table!

The partition editor can be useful, if, for some reason, your hard disk no longer boots (Figure 18.4). Then—if all other means fail and your only alternative is to format the disk and lose data—you can try making a partition bootable again.

To do this, select the line for the first DOS partition and move the marking bar to the first column. Using the spacebar, you may now switch between the different partition states. When the designation "DOS-16" appears, you may have reached the correct state again. Store the table after answering the usual questions.

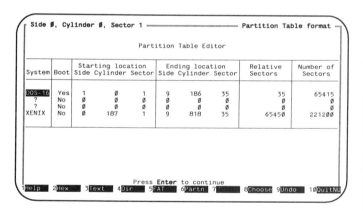

Figure 18.4: The partition editor in the Advanced Editions

Step 19:

Batch Programs

The utilities for improving batch programs have a strange history. In the beginning there was the small BEEP program that was used to produce a tone. It is still available in its original form in version 3.x. In version 4.0, BEEP became a minimal music program with which the user can play tone sequences.

Then, the ASK program was added, which made interactive prompting in batch programs possible. Finally, version 4.5 combined BEEP and ASK to form the utility BE (Batch Enhancer). With this program, you can make batch programs into bona fide applications.

This step introduces all these programs. The step begins with BEEP and ASK from version 4.0 and then describes the BE program and its capabilities. You should allow 30 minutes for this topic.

The BEEP Program

BEEP in version 3.x can be explained quickly. You run the program and then hear a tone. That's about all. Despite this, BEEP is suitable in this version for use in batch files. For example, in batch programs that run for a long time, you can create a beep at the end to announce the completion of the program.

In version 4.0, BEEP can generate entire sequences of tones. In this manner, you can create short musical compositions as batch programs. You specify what tone is to be heard, for how long, and how often using the four possible switches:

BEEP as a tone generator

/F100   The program generates a tone of 100 Hz. You may use any value—if the program cannot generate a tone of the specified frequency, BEEP selects the default tone.

/D9   The program generates a tone for 9/18 of a second. You may use any value.

/R2   The program repeats the tone twice. You may use any value.

/W9   The program pauses for 9/18 (nine eighteenths) of a second between tones. You may use any value.

This small batch file produces a type of scale:

```
ECHO OFF
FOR %%X in (262 294 330 368 392 440
498 536) DO BEEP /F%%X
```

BEEP
processes
a tone file

Of course, you can only generate one tone at a time interactively. You can construct files of longer tone sequences for BEEP. The sample file MARY of the Norton Utilities version 4.0 demonstrates this. Here is an excerpt:

```
/F330 /D5
/F294 /D1
/F262 /D3
/F294 /D3
/R2 /F330 /D3
/F330 /D8
/R2 /F294 /D3
/F294 /D8
```

You can play a tone file like this by calling BEEP with the filename. For example,

```
BEEP MARY
```

The ASK Program

Anyone who frequently writes batch programs knows how useful an interactive capability would be. While you can draw conclusions about user input by querying the so-called Error Levels, this method is far from convenient.

Interaction becomes very simple with ASK. You can use the program like any other batch command—just like BEEP. You must also specify two switches. The first switch is the question to be asked with ASK. You may use any phase whatsoever in this question as long as you enclose the phase in quotation marks. (You may also use quotation marks within the question.) The second switch is a list of the keys to be accepted as valid responses.

An example will clarify this. This example shows an ASK application in a small menu:

```
ASK "Start which program? -> ", WSDQ
```

This example provides four choices—W for word processing, S for spreadsheet, D for database, and Q for quit, the command to exit the menu.

If the user presses a key not contained in the list, ASK responds with an error tone. You use the Error Level to determine which key the user pressed. Each key is assigned an Error Level corresponding to the position of the key in the list. In the example above, pressing **W** sets the Error Level to 1, **S** to 2, **D** to 3, and **Q** to 4.

You then make use of Error Level to provide additional control. A complete example below makes this clear:

```
ECHO OFF
:START
CLS
ECHO Word processing (MS Word)
ECHO Spreadsheet (Lotus 1-2-3)
ECHO Database (Q&A 3.0)
ECHO .
ECHO Quit
ECHO .
ASK "Start which program? -> ", WSDQ
IF ERRORLEVEL 4 GOTO QUIT
```

```
IF ERRORLEVEL 3 GOTO DATABASE
IF ERRORLEVEL 2 GOTO SPREADSHEET
IF ERRORLEVEL 1 GOTO WORDPROC
GOTO START
:WORDPROC
CD C:\WORD
WORD
CD \NORTON
GOTO START
:SPREADSHEET
CD C:\LOTUS123
123
CD \NORTON
GOTO START
:DATABASE
CD C:\QA
QA
CD \NORTON
GOTO START
:QUIT
EXIT
```

You may use any of the character keys in the key list. However, you may not use the arrow keys. You may not use the PgDn, PgUp, Home, or End key; the function keys, the Return, Tab, Del, Ins, or Backspace key, or the spacebar, either. If you do not specify a key list, the program accepts any key press as input. This means that after the user presses any key, the program continues. Figure 19.1 shows the batch program running.

You should keep two things in mind. Always query the key presses or the Error Level of these presses in reverse order. This is because in batch programs the levels have decreasing priorities. This means that the program executes a condition for Error Level 4 only if it finds no conditions for Error Levels 3, 2, or 1 first. The second note concerns the sample batch programs. Following each program name, always enter the directory containing the batch files. In the example, this is the C:\NORTON directory. For you it may be a different directory.

```
Word processing (MS Word)
Spreadsheet (Lotus 1-2-3)
Database (Q&A 3.0)
.
Quit
.
Start which program? ->
```

Figure 19.1: A sample batch program using the ASK command

The BE Program

You will not find BEEP or ASK in version 4.5. Both have become options in a program providing an abundance of capabilities. BE operates like BEEP. You may call it either with a
command and switches or you can have the program read the
commands with their switches from a file. The second method
is particularly attractive if you wish to execute several commands one after another.

BE Commands

The following list contains all BE commands and how they
are used:

ASK   Works in the manner already described.

BE   Works in the manner already described.

BOX   With BOX, you draw rectangles on the screen. You
         must specify the position of the top left corner and
         the position of the bottom right corner. As a last
         switch, you may specify the color of the rectangle.
         For example, "BE BOX 10,10,20,30,7".

CLS   You erase the screen with CLS.

DELAY	With DELAY, you can specify a pause between two actions. The program measures this pause in ticks. One tick corresponds to 1/18 of a second. For example, "BE DELAY 36".
PRINTCHAR	The PRINTCHAR command prints a character on the screen. With this command, you may specify how often the character is to be repeated. For example, "BE PRINTCHAR *80".
ROWCOL	With ROWCOL, you move the cursor to a specific position and put a phrase there. If you do not specify a phrase, the program stores only the cursor position. As the final switch, you specify the text color. For example, "BE ROWCOL 10,10,Cursor,12".
SA .	You use the SA command like the SA program (see Step 4).
WINDOW	This command is similar to the BOX command. The difference is that a WINDOW covers the existing screen contents whereas a BOX provides a frame. The switches are identical. Two effects are added: EXPLODE and SHADOW. For example, "BE WINDOW 1,1,20,70,15 EXPLODE".

 Incidentally, all switches may be separated from one another with commas or blanks. Any text longer than one word must be enclosed in quotation marks.

Step 20:

Miscellaneous

You will learn about two small utilities in this last step, TM (Time Mark) and LP (Line Print). The usefulness of these utilities is often underestimated. While you may use LP as a substitute for the DOS PRINT function, TM has no equivalent.

Both programs can be explained quickly. For this reason, you will need only 15 minutes to work on this step.

The TM program

You already learned about one portion of the TM program in Step 4 if you own version 4.5. In that step, you saw how you can set the time and date, and how to work with the four stop-watches using the NCC program.

With TM, the system date and time are always available. If you run TM without switches, they will be displayed at the right of the next line. The date and time are output like this:

```
1:30 pm, Wednesday, May 31, 1990
```

Access to system date and time

When running TM, you can also provide a commenting text. If, for example, you run TM this way:

```
TM "It is now"
```

the program will display the following:

```
It is now 1:30 pm, Wednesday, May 31, 1990
```

Take care to enclose the comment in quotation marks because otherwise only the first word will be used.

You can move the output to the left side of the screen with the /L switch. The /LOG switch prepares the screen output for the printer. Using this switch and redirecting the output, you can stamp the date and time on a printout. The following command

```
TM "As of: " /L/LOG > PRN
```

places the system date and time left-justified on the first line of a page to be printed. Of course, you can also time-stamp files.

The following command appends a line containing the system date and time to the file LETTER.DAT.

```
TM "As of: " /L/LOG >> LETTER.DAT
```

Stopwatches

TM maintains four independent watches. These can be controlled individually with the /C1 to /C4 switches. Two commands act as control elements. Use START to reset a watch to 0 and start it. Use STOP to stop the watch and output the elapsed time (in seconds). A stop command does not reset the stopwatches. The time continues to run and can be called up in a cumulative fashion. You do not reset the watch to 0 until the next start command.

Stop commands display the date and time by default. You can suppress this display with the /N switch. As you might expect, you can move the stopwatch displays to the left on the screen (with /L), and you can format them as printer output with /LOG and redirect them to the printer or to a file.

The LP program

With the LP (Line Print) program, you can print files or redirect them to a print file. In so doing, you can affect the form of the printout. You can even print several files in one operation if you can define the desired group of files with wildcards in the file names. The following command causes all TXT files in the TEXT directory to be printed:

```
LP C:\TEXT\*.TXT
```

Besides the file or group of files to be printed, you must also specify the output device. If you do not specify anything, the data are sent to the standard printer (usually the printer connected to port LPT1). However, you can also specify any other printer ports or the serial interface(s). Printing via the serial interface also makes data transfer possible.

Switches

A complete series of switches are available for LP. First consider the general switches:

/N   The program numbers each line. The serial
            number precedes the text.

/WS   The program prints a text file produced using
            WordStar with all formatting.

/EBCDIC   The program uses the EBCDIC code.

/N is particularly important for printing lists, tables, and similar files.

The next group of switches influences the appearance of the file during printing:

/H66   The page is 66 lines long.
/W85   The page is 85 characters wide.
/T3   The top margin is three lines high.
/B5   The bottom margin is five lines high.
/L5   The left margin is five characters wide.
/R5   The right margin is five characters wide.
/S1   The page is single-spaced.
/80   The program prints 80 characters per line.
/132   The program prints 132 characters per line.

The values used above happen to be the defaults that LP uses if you do not specify the corresponding switches. As continuous paper is usually 72 lines long, you often must specify /H72.

With the following switch, you specify the starting number for page numbering:

/P1   The program numbers the first page 1.

The following switch is particularly powerful. You can specify values of 0 to 2 for it:

/HEADER0   The program prints no header lines.

/HEADER1   The program prints one header line containing the following information: name of the file, date and time in TM format, page number.

/HEADER2   The program prints two header lines. The top line contains the same information as that for the /HEADER1 switch. The second line accommodates the creation date and time of the file to be printed.

In cases where special formatting is required or desired, you can even transmit printer control characters. These control characters must be stored in a file sent to the printer before the real printout of LP. The format of the control codes corresponds to that used by Lotus 1-2-3. You send the control file to the printer with the following switch:

```
/SET:CTRL.CDS
```

Of course, you must specify the appropriate file name after the colon. You enter the codes as three-digit decimal numbers in the control file. Each code must start with a backslash. For example, for Epson printers, you switch on bold printing like this:

```
\027\069
```

You could store these codes, for example, in a file named BOLD.CDS. With the command

```
LP C:\TEXTS\*.TXT /SET:BOLD.CDS
```

all TXT files will be printed out using bold print (on an Epson printer or compatible).

Index

A

Advanced Editions, 4
  directory manipulation with, 102–103
  partition editing with, 115
Alt key for settings, 111
ANSI driver, 19, 98
archive attribute, 83–84
arrow keys, 7–9, 106
ASCII characters, 107–108
ASK program, 118–121
asterisks (*)
  for cursor, 23
  for keyboard settings, 25
  as wildcard character, 67
attributes
  file, 83–85, 100–101
  screen, 19–21
AUTOEXEC.BAT file
  copying of, 85
  modification of, 2, 4, 93

B

background color, 20–21, 24, 98, 111
backing up of original disks, 1–2
backslashes (\) with LP, 126
bad clusters
  and DT program, 29–30
  map of, 99
  marking of, 31, 45–47
base 16 number system, 105–109
batch programs, 19, 117–122
BE (Batch Enhancer) program, 19, 121–122
BEEP program, 117–118
bit copies, 114–115
blanks
  in file names, 102
  in volume names, 40
blinking attribute, 20
bold attribute, 20

boot sector
  editing of, 112–113
  and formatting, 55–56
  and NDD, 45
bootable disks, making of, 47–48
bootable partitions, making of, 115
border color, 24
BOX command, 121
bright attribute, 20

C

case-sensitivity with text searches, 69
CD command (DOS), substitute for, 94–95
characters, screen, representation of, 19–21
CLS command, 121
clusters
  copying of, 114–115
  in disk map, 99
  and DT, 29–30
  editing of, 112–114
  and FAT, 72–76
  marking of bad, 31, 45–47
  and optimization, 49–53
  starting, 78–79, 100–103, 106
colons (:) with LP, 126
color, screen, 20–21, 24, 98, 111
comments for files, 87–89
Complete Format mode, 36
CONFIG.SYS file
  ANSI driver in, 19
  copying of, 85
control characters in printer files, 126–127
copy-protection, 115
copying
  of AUTOEXEC.BAT and CONFIG.SYS
    files, 85
  of files, 114–115
  of original disks, 1–2
CPU speed, measuring of, 13–15

FD (File Date/Time) program, 86–87
FF (File Find) program, 65–67
FI (File Info) program, 87–89
File Allocation Table
  editing of, 114
  and erased files, 73–79
  and formatting, 55–56
  and NDD, 45
  number of, 16–17
  and optimization, 49
  and QU, 80
  and safe formatting, 33, 36
  and sectors, 72
File Attributes program, 83–85
File Date/Time program, 86–87
File Find program, 65–67
File Info program, 87–89
File Size program, 85–86
files
  attributes for, 83–85, 100–101
  copying of, 114–115
  date and time stamps for, 86–87,
    100–102
  deleted, recovery of, ix, 71–80
  deleted, security of, 40–41
  directories for, 72–74
  executable, text changes in, 108
  fragmentation of, 49–53, 99
  listing of, 9, 59–61, 87–89
  moving of, 64
  names for, changing of, 102
  printing of, 124–127
  searching for, 65–67
  size of, 72, 85–86, 100–101
  sorting of, 59–64
finding of data, 65–69
floppy disks
  defective, 27–31
  formatting of, 33–37
  installation of Norton Utilities on, 2–3
  media descriptor for, 16
foreground color, 20–21, 24, 98
FORMAT.EXE program, replacement of, 4
Format Recovery program, 55–58
formatting
  of backup disks, 1
  recovering from, 55–58
  safe, 4, 33–37
FR (Format Recovery) program, 55–58
fragmentation of files, 49–53, 99
FRECOVER files, 56–57

FS (File Size) program, 85–86
function keys, 9–10, 111

G

General failure errors, recovery from, 49
graphic display of directories, 60–61, 95–96

H

hard disk drives
  editing of, 39–41
  formatting of, 36
  installation of Norton Utilities on, 3–4
  media descriptor for, 16
  operating speed of, 14
  optimization of, 49–53
  recovery of data on, 55–58
  testing of, 30
header lines, 126
help, function key for, 10
hex editor and hexadecimal numbers,
  105–109
hidden attribute, 83–84
Home key, 8, 101–102, 106

I

INSTALL.EXE program, 1, 3–4
installation of Norton Utilities, 1–5
Integrator, 10–12
intensity, screen, 20–21
interactive batch programs, 118–121
interface, user, 7–12

K

key functions, 9–10
keyboard, repetition rate for, 24–25
keys, sorting, 61–62

L

labels, volume, 39–40
LD (List Directory) program, 59–61
Line Print program, 124–127
List Directory program, 59–61
listing of directories and files, 9, 59–61,
  66, 87–89
logical disk drives, 98

Logical Disk Information, 45–46
logical units, 72
LP (Line Print) program, 124–127

M

maintenance programs
    NDD, 43–49
    SD, 49–53
map, disk, 99
marking of bad clusters, 31, 45–47
MD command (DOS), substitute for, 94–95
media descriptor, 16
memory, occupied, 14–15
menus, 7–9
minus sign (–)
    with attributes, 85
    with directory sorting, 62–63
moving of files, 64

N

names
    file, changing of, 102
    volume disk, 39–40
NCC (Norton Control Center) program,
    21–26
NCD (Norton Change Directory) program,
    93–96
NDD (Norton Disk Doctor) program, 43–49
Norton, Peter, ix
NORTON.BAK directory, 3
Norton Change Directory program, 93–96
Norton Control Center program, 21–26
Norton Disk Companion, 17
Norton Disk Doctor program, 43–49
Norton Integrator, 10–12
NU (Norton Utility) program, 71–79
    for disk analysis, 97–103
    editing data with, 105–109
    menus for, 8–9

O

operating speed, measuring of, 13–15
optimization, disk, 49–53

P

page numbering, 126
palettes, 24

parameters, Integrator, 12
partitions, editing of, 115
pauses with BE, 122
performance index (PI), 14
PgDn and PgUp keys, 8, 106
Physical Disk Information, 45–46
plus sign (+)
    with attributes, 85
    with directory sorting, 63
ports, setting of, 25
preventive maintenance, 43–49
Print mode, 111
PRINTCHAR command, 122
printing
    with BE, 122
    of directory lists, 60
    of files, 124–127

Q

QU (Quick UnErase) program, 79–81
question mark (?) as wildcard character, 67
quick compression of clusters, 51
Quick Format mode, 36
Quick UnErase program, 79–81
quitting, function key for, 10
quotation marks (")
    with ASK program, 119
    with TM, 123
    for volume names, 40

R

RAM, free, 14–15
RD command (DOS), substitute for, 94–95
read-only attribute, 83–84
recovery of disk data, 71–81
    directories, 77–79, 91–92
    on hard disks, 55–58
    with NDD, 48
    and WipeDisk, 40
rectangles with BE, 121
repetition rate, keyboard, 24–25
reverse video, 20
root directory, 72–73
ROWCOL command, 122

S

SA (Screen Attributes) program, 19–21
Safe Format program, 4, 33–37